GLENCOE PHYSICS
Principles and Problems

Supplemental Problems

Glencoe McGraw-Hill

New York, New York   Columbus, Ohio   Woodland Hills, California   Peoria, Illinois

GLENCOE
PHYSICS
Principles and Problems

Student Edition
Teacher Wraparound Edition
Teacher Classroom Resources

Transparency Package with Transparency Masters
Laboratory Manual SE and TE
Physics Lab and Pocket Lab Worksheets
Study Guide SE and TE
Chapter Assessment
Tech Prep Applications
Critical Thinking
Reteaching
Enrichment
Physics Skills
Supplemental Problems
Problems and Solutions Manual
Spanish Resources
Lesson Plans with block scheduling
Reviewing Physics

Technology

TestCheck Software (Win/Mac)
MindJogger Videoquizzes
Interactive Student Edition
Interactive Teacher Edition
Interactive Lesson Planner
Website at *science.glencoe.com*
Physics for the Computer Age CD-ROM (Win/Mac)

The Glencoe Science Professional Development Series

Graphing Calculators in the Science Classroom
Cooperative Learning in the Science Classroom
Alternate Assessment in the Science Classroom
Performance Assessment in the Science Classroom
Lab and Safety Skills in the Science Classroom

Glencoe/McGraw-Hill
A Division of The McGraw-Hill Companies

Copyright © by the McGraw-Hill Companies, Inc. All rights reserved. Permission is granted to reproduce the material contained herein on the condition that such material be reproduced only for classroom use; be provided to students, teachers, and families without charge; and be used solely in conjunction with the **Physics: Principles and Problems** program. Any other reproduction, for use or sale, is prohibited without prior written permission of the publisher.

Send all inquiries to:
Glencoe/McGraw-Hill
8787 Orion Place
Columbus, Ohio 43240

ISBN 0-07-826608-4
Printed in the United States of America.

2 3 4 5 6 7 8 9   024   07 06 05 04 03 02

Contents

To the Teacher iv

Title	Page

- **2** A Mathematical Toolkit 1
- **3** Describing Motion 3
- **4** Vector Addition 5
- **5** A Mathematical Model of Motion 7
- **6** Forces 9
- **7** Forces and Motion in Two Dimensions . 11
- **8** Universal Gravitation 13
- **9** Momentum and Its Conservation 15
- **10** Energy, Work, and Simple Machines . . . 17
- **11** Energy 19
- **12** Thermal Energy 21
- **13** States of Matter 23
- **14** Waves and Energy Transfer 25
- **15** Sound 27
- **16** Light 29
- **17** Reflection and Refraction 31
- **18** Mirrors and Lenses 33
- **19** Diffraction and Interference of Light . . . 35
- **20** Static Electricity 37
- **21** Electric Fields 39
- **22** Current Electricity 41
- **23** Series and Parallel Circuits 43
- **24** Magnetic Fields 45
- **25** Electromagnetic Induction 47
- **26** Electromagnetism 49
- **27** Quantum Theory 51
- **28** The Atom 53
- **29** Solid State Electronics 55
- **30** The Nucleus 57
- **31** Nuclear Applications 59

Answer Key 61

To the Teacher

The *Supplemental Problems* booklet contains additional problems for Chapters 2–31. You can assign those problems whenever extra practice is required. Complete solutions and answers are provided in the back of the booklet, making this a valuable source for both students and teachers.

2 A Mathematical Toolkit

1. Express the following quantities in scientific notation.
   a. 22 300 kg
   b. 401 kg
   c. 0.57 kg
   d. 0.000 084 kg
   e. 0.000 000 044 9 kg

2. Convert each of the following measurements as directed.
   a. 11 m to cm
   b. 230 ms to s
   c. 0.133 kg to g
   d. 8.5 dm to cm

3. Solve the following problems and express the answers in scientific notation.
   a. 32.1 cm + 2.1 cm
   b. 4×10^3 kg + 3×10^3 kg
   c. 8.9×10^2 mm + 3.4×10^2 mm
   d. 63.0×10^2 ms − 21×10^1 ms
   e. 59×10^1 m − 0.20 km

4. Find the value of each of the following quantities and express it in scientific notation.
   a. $(2.00 \times 10^1 \text{ mm})(2.10 \times 10^1 \text{ mm})(2.20 \times 10^1 \text{ mm})$
   b. $(6.96 \times 10^2 \text{ kg})(1.2 \times 10^{-1} \text{ m/s})$
   c. $\dfrac{35.84 \times 10^3 \text{ m}}{56 \text{ s}}$
   d. $\dfrac{(2.5 \times 10^{-2} \text{ kg}) \times (1.7 \times 10^{-2} \text{ m})}{(8.5 \times 10^{-5} \text{ s})}$
   e. $\dfrac{(4.2 \times 10^1 \text{ kg})}{(3.5 \times 10^4 \text{ cm})(2.0 \times 10^2 \text{ dm})(1.5 \times 10^{-1} \text{ m})}$

5. State the number of significant digits in each measurement and express the value in scientific notation.
   a. 110 m
   b. 0.2°C
   c. 0.090 11 kg
   d. 52.5×10^{-3} mm
   e. 600.0 N
   f. 20.40 m/s
   g. 0.71 ns
   h. 0.06 kg
   i. 7040 m

6. Add or subtract as indicated and express the answer in scientific notation with the correct number of significant digits.
   a. 9902 m + 201 m
   b. 5.060 cm + 32.07 cm
   c. 1.5 km − 355 m
   d. 5.5×10^{-1} mm + 2×10^{-3} cm

Physics: Principles and Problems

2 A Mathematical Toolkit

7. Evaluate the following quantities and state each answer in scientific notation with the correct number of significant digits.
   a. $(4.2 \times 10^1 \text{ m})^2$
   b. 1200 m/10.0 s
   c. (17 mm)(17.6 cm)
   d. 0.1387 kg/[(0.121 m)(0.021 m)(2.00 m)]

8. Table 2-1 shows the volume of blood delivered at various intervals during a routine blood transfusion.

   TABLE 2-1

Time ($\times 10^2$ s)	Volume (cm³)
0.00	0.0
1.00	6.0
2.00	12.1
3.00	17.9
4.00	23.9
5.00	29.9
6.00	35.9

   a. Plot the values given in the table and draw the curve that best fits all points.
   b. Describe the resulting curve.
   c. Use the graph to write an equation relating volume to time.
   d. In how many minutes will 5.00×10^2 cm³ of blood transfuse at this rate?

9. In an experiment, a student dropped tiny aluminum spheres of varying radii into a tall cylinder of glycerin and then measured the speed at which they fell. Table 2-2 shows the data.

   TABLE 2-2

Sphere radius ($\times 10^{-2}$ m)	Maximum speed ($\times 10^2$ m/s)
0.20	0.15
0.40	0.61
0.60	1.35
0.80	2.42
1.00	3.79

   a. Plot the values given in the table and draw the curve that best fits all points.
   b. The equation of the line is $s = ar^2$, where a is a constant for glycerin and aluminum. Describe the curve.
   c. What is the numerical value of a?
   d. What are the units of a?

10. If small-diameter glass tubes, called capillary tubes, are placed in water, the water rises in the tubes. Table 2-3 shows the radii of the capillary tubes and the average height that the water rose in each tube.

    TABLE 2-3

Radius ($\times 10^{-5}$ m)	Height of water column ($\times 10^{-2}$ m)
2.0	72.5
4.0	36.2
6.0	24.2
8.0	18.1
10.0	14.3

    a. Plot the values given in the table and draw the curve that best fits all points.
    b. Describe the resulting curve.
    c. According to the graph, what is the relationship between the height to which the water rises and the radius of the capillary tube?
    d. Write the equation relating the height of the water column and the radius of the capillary tube. Give the value of the constant to three significant digits.
    e. What are the units of c?

3 Describing Motion

1. A truck is traveling at a constant speed as shown below.

   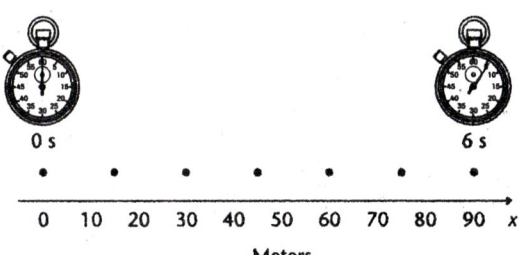

   Sketch the motion diagram on a separate piece of paper and draw the displacements of the truck at 2 seconds and 5 seconds. Label the displacements d_0 and d_1, respectively. Draw and label the displacement, Δd, that the truck underwent from 2 to 5 seconds.

2. The motion diagrams below represent an SUV and a car each traveling in the same direction.

   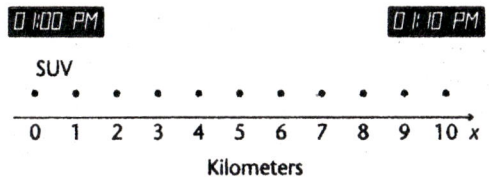

   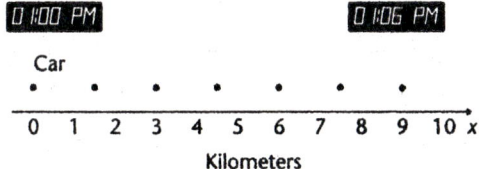

   Sketch the motion diagrams on a separate piece of paper and answer the following questions.

   a. Which vehicle has the greater speed? How do you know?

   b. Draw the displacement of each vehicle after 4 seconds and the vector representing the displacement of the car with respect to the SUV.

   c. The SUV and car are traveling in opposite directions with the same speeds as before. Draw and label the displacement of each vehicle 3 seconds after they pass each other. Assume the SUV is traveling in the positive x-direction to the right. Then draw the vector representing the displacement of the car with respect to the SUV at 3 seconds.

   d. Redraw your answers to Problem 2c assuming the car is traveling in the positive x-direction to the left.

   e. Compare the magnitude of the vector representing the displacement of the car with respect to the SUV with the magnitude of the vector representing the displacement of the SUV with respect to the car at 3 seconds.

For Questions 3–6, create pictorial and physical models. Do not solve the problems.

3. A helicopter ascends at a constant speed of 5 m/s. How far does it rise in 5 seconds?

4. An empty toy wagon reaches the bottom of a hill and rolls onto the level ground at a speed of 1.5 m/s. How long will it take the wagon to come to a stop if its acceleration is -0.6 m/s^2?

5. A diver jumps vertically with a velocity of 4.0 m/s from a platform and enters the water 1.9 seconds later. How high is the platform? (Hint: The acceleration is the same whether the diver is moving up or down.)

6. A driver backs a car at a velocity of -2.3 m/s from a driveway onto a street. If the acceleration of the car is 0.8 m/s^2, how far onto the street does the car move before it comes to a stop?

Physics: Principles and Problems

4 Vector Addition

1. A soccer player runs forward a distance of 4 m, reverses direction and runs a distance of 3 m, and then reverses direction again and runs a distance of 8 m.
   a. What distance does the player run?
   b. What is his displacement?

2. A jogger starts a three-part jog by running 0.24 km north, then 0.16 km east, and finally back to her starting point along a straight-line path. Graphically determine the jogger's third displacement.

3. After takeoff, an air-traffic controller locates a small plane 12.0 km southeast of the airport. At this point, the plane turns 20.0° to the east of its original flight path and flies 21.0 km. What is the magnitude of the plane's displacement from the airport?

4. A gymnast tumbles forward 4.0 m, does cartwheels to the left for 6.0 m, and climbs a vertical rope to a height of 3.0 m. What is the magnitude of the gymnast's displacement?

5. Graphically determine the difference in displacement, Δd, for each pair of displacements below.
   a. $d_1 = +2.0$ m, $d_2 = +3.0$ m
   b. $d_1 = +2.0$ m, $d_2 = +2.0$ m
   c. $d_1 = +2.0$ m, $d_2 = -2.0$ m
   d. $d_1 = 2.0$ m at 35° north of east
   $d_2 = 3.0$ m at 25° south of east

6. Two cars approach a crossroad 36 m ahead. Car A is traveling east at 9 m/s and car B is traveling south at 12 m/s.
   a. What is the location of car B relative to car A?
   b. What is the location of car B relative to car A 2.0 seconds later?
   c. Where does the car that first reaches the crossroad locate the other car the moment the former passes through the crossroad?

7. The moving sidewalk at an airport has a speed of 0.9 m/s toward the departure gate.
   a. A man is walking toward the departure gate on the moving sidewalk at a speed of 1.0 m/s relative to the sidewalk. What is the velocity of the man relative to a woman standing off the moving sidewalk?
   b. On a similar moving sidewalk moving in the opposite direction, a child walks toward the terminal at a speed of 0.4 m/s relative to the sidewalk. What is the velocity of the man relative to the child?

8. A kite is tethered to a stake on a beach. The wind has a constant velocity of 16 km/h at an angle of 15° from the horizontal relative to the beach. Find the components of the kite's velocity relative to the wind.

9. A hiker starts by walking along a straight path. He then turns and walks 260.0 m west. If he finds he is located 360.0 m exactly north of his starting point, what was his displacement along the path?

10. A hammer slides down a roof that makes a 40.0° angle with the horizontal. What are the magnitudes of the components of the hammer's velocity at the edge of the roof if it is moving at a speed of 4.25 m/s?

Physics: Principles and Problems Supplemental Problems • Chapter 4

5 A Mathematical Model of Motion

1. A biker starts a trip and rides at a constant velocity of +12 km/h for 0.20 h. For the next 0.10 h he bikes at an increased constant velocity and finds that he is at a rest stop +4.8 km from his starting point. In the next 0.20 h, half of which he rests, his average velocity is +9.0 km/h.

   a. Construct a *d*-*t* graph for the trip.

   b. What is his average velocity for the trip?

2. Alice and Faye are located +18 m from a flagpole. They begin running with constant velocities of −2.0 m/s and −3.0 m/s, respectively. At 10.0 s, Faye changes her velocity and meets Alice 3.0 seconds later.

   a. Plot the motion of each girl on the same *d*-*t* graph.

   b. Where do they meet?

   c. What is Faye's average velocity for the last 3.0 seconds?

3. Seth starts a half-hour canoe trip by paddling at a velocity of +5.0 km/h relative to the river for 0.20 h. He rests for 0.05 h and then paddles at a velocity of −3.0 km/h relative to the river for the remainder of the half hour.

   a. Construct a *d*-*t* graph of his motion.

   b. Construct a *d*-*t* graph of Seth's motion relative to the shore if he paddles upstream in a river that has a velocity of +2.0 km/h. On the same graph plot Seth's motion if he paddles downstream in the same river.

4. One day a rabbit challenged a skunk to a race. The following *v*-*t* graph shows the motion of a crazy rabbit during the race.

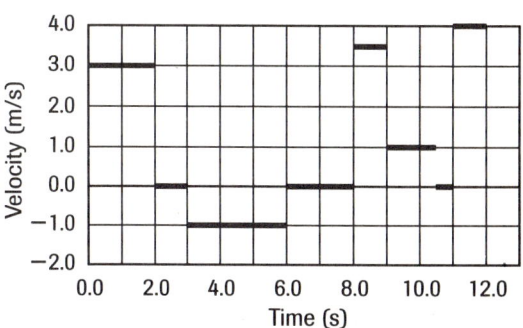

   If the rabbit crosses the finish line at 12.0 s, what average velocity did the skunk maintain to cross the finish line a moment before the rabbit?

5. Look at the *v*-*t* graph of a remote-controlled toy car below. At *t* = 0.0 s, the car is located at = +10.0 cm.

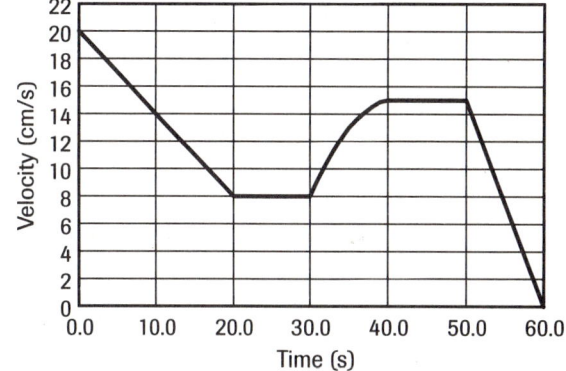

   a. In which time interval or intervals does the car have a constant velocity?

   b. In which time interval or intervals does the car have constant positive acceleration?

5 A Mathematical Model of Motion

c. In which time interval or intervals does the car have constant negative acceleration?

d. In which time interval or intervals is the car moving forward?

e. What is the magnitude of the acceleration at $t = 35.0$ s?

6. A golf ball leaves a tee at a speed of 2.0×10^2 km/h after being accelerated for 0.56 ms.

   a. What is the ball's average acceleration in m/s^2?

   b. How far does it move in this time interval?

7. A flea develops an acceleration of 2.0×10^3 m/s^2 during takeoff. After takeoff the flea reaches a height of 36 mm.

   a. How fast does the flea leave the ground?

   b. How long does the take-off acceleration last?

8. While descending at a constant speed of 1.0 m/s, a scuba diver releases a cork, which accelerates upward at 3.0 m/s^2. What is the diver's depth when the cork reaches the surface 2.0 s later?

9. A car with a velocity of +27 m/s slows down at a rate of -8.5 m/s^2 to a stop in a distance of 43 m on a dry road. The same car traveling at +27 m/s slows down at a rate of -6.5 m/s^2 to a stop on a wet road.

   a. How much farther does the car travel on the wet road before coming to a stop?

   b. What maximum car speed will allow the car traveling on the wet road to stop in a distance of 43 m?

10. The engine of a toy rocket supplies an average acceleration of 38.0 m/s^2 to the rocket for an interval of 0.80 s.

    a. If the toy rocket is launched vertically, how high does it rise in this interval?

    b. How fast is the rocket moving at the end of 0.80 s?

    c. What altitude does the rocket reach before falling back to Earth?

    d. How long does it take the rocket to reach this altitude?

6 Forces

1. The propellers of a small airplane produce a forward thrust of 6.2×10^4 N on the plane which has a mass of 2.8×10^4 kg. What is the plane's forward acceleration?

2. If the plane in Problem 1 is flying horizontally, what is the lift (upward force of air) on the plane?

3. A girl in a canoe uses a paddle to push the canoe at rest from a dock giving it a speed of 0.30 m/s. If the paddle is in contact with the dock for 0.75 seconds, what is the average force on the canoe? (The mass of the canoe is 27 kg and that of the girl is 52 kg.)

4. A student attaches a spring scale to a 2.30-kg book and then releases the book. If the student maintains a scale reading of 25.0 N, what is the magnitude and direction of the book's acceleration? (Assume upward is the positive direction.)

5. If the student in problem 4 maintains a scale reading of 22.0 N, what will be the displacement of the book in 1.0 s?

6. Two laboratory masses are tied to opposite ends of a weightless string, which passes over a frictionless pulley as shown below.

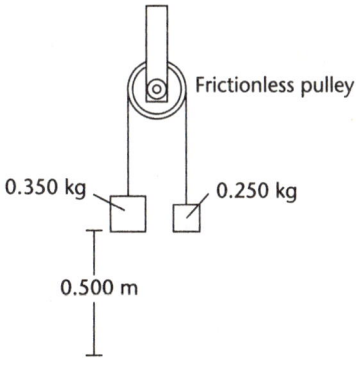

   a. If the masses are released from rest, what is the acceleration of the 0.250-kg mass?

   b. After the masses are released, how long will it take the 0.350 kg mass to strike the floor?

   c. A student decides to demonstrate this problem. After setting up the equipment, she accurately measures the time it takes the 0.350-kg mass to reach the floor as 0.92 s. If she attributes the cause of the difference in times to the frictional force on the pulley, what is the size of this force?

7. A horse is pulling two loaded sleds across the snow. The first sled, which has a mass of 250 kg, is attached to the horse by a harness that can withstand a maximum tension of 4500 N. The second sled, which has a mass of 150 kg, is attached to the first sled by a rope that can withstand a maximum tension of 450 N.

   a. What is the acceleration of the sleds just before the rope snaps?

   b. What is the tension in the harness just before the rope snaps?

8. A pendulum with a length of 1.00 m is in a rocket that is far removed from any gravitational effects. If the rocket is accelerating as shown below, what is the period of the pendulum?

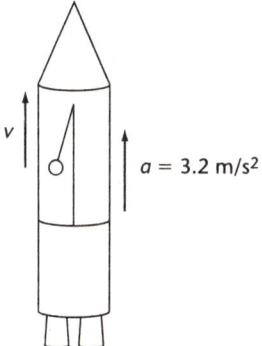

Physics: Principles and Problems

6 Forces

9. A 65.0-kg passenger in a car is securely fastened in a safety belt as shown below.

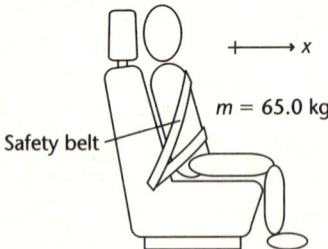

Calculate the magnitude and determine the direction of the horizontal force that the safety belt and seat exert on the passenger for each of the following conditions. (Assume the car is moving only horizontally.)

a. $v_0 = +20.0$ m/s, $a = 0$ m/s^2
b. $v_0 = +20.0$ m/s, $a = +1.50$ m/s^2
c. $v_0 = 10.0$ m/s, $a = -3.00$ m/s^2
d. $v_0 = -3.0$ m/s, $a = -1.20$ m/s^2
e. $v_0 = -10.0$ m/s, $a = +2.3$ m/s^2

10. In Problem 9, the car is traveling at 20.0 m/s and the driver suddenly slows down the car at a rate of 5.00 m/s^2.

a. What is the magnitude and direction of the force that the passenger exerts on the safety belt and seat?

b. After slowing down, the driver accelerates the car forward at a rate of 1.50 m/s^2. What is the magnitude and direction of the force that the passenger exerts on the safety belt and seat?

7 Forces and Motion in Two Dimensions

1. A dog tugs forward with force of 28 N on a taut leash at an angle of 15° from the horizontal. What is the magnitude of the tension in the leash?

2. A rod supports a 2.35-kg lamp as shown below.

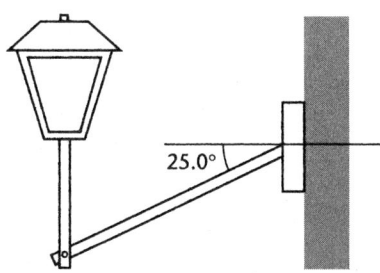

   a. What is the magnitude of the tension in the rod?

   b. Calculate the components of the force that the bracket exerts on the rod?

3. A 20.0-N box is resting on a frictionless surface as shown below.

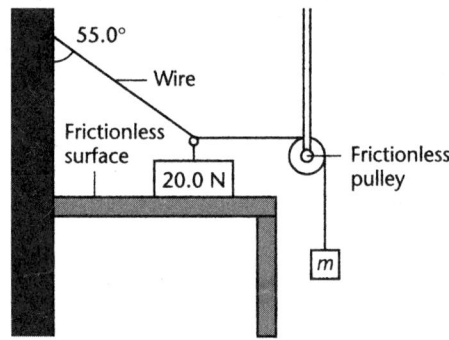

   a. If the magnitude of the tension in the wire is 12.0 N, what is the value of the mass, m?

   b. The table supporting the box is removed and the height of the pulley is adjusted so that the string connecting mass, m, and the box remains parallel to the floor. What is the magnitude and orientation of the tension in the wire?

4. A 25.0-kg crate has an adjustable handle so that it can be pushed or pulled by the handle at various angles.

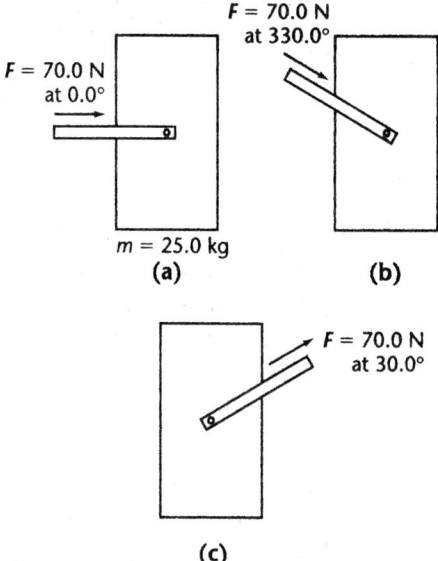

   Determine the acceleration of the crate for each situation shown in the diagram knowing that the coefficient of sliding friction between the floor and the bottom of the crate is 0.20.

5. A child shoves a small toboggan weighing 100.0-N up a snowy hill, giving the toboggan an initial speed of 6.0 m/s. If the hill is inclined at an angle of 32° above the horizontal, how far along the hill will the toboggan slide? Assume the coefficient of sliding friction between the toboggan and the snow is 0.15.

6. A nozzle in a fountain is angled 23° below the horizontal and is located 2.0 m above the edge of the basin. If the water is ejected at a speed of 4.2 m/s from the nozzle, how far from the edge of the basin does the water fall?

Physics: Principles and Problems   Supplemental Problems • Chapter 7   11

7 Forces and Motion in Two Dimensions

7. A juggler tosses a ball from his right hand to his left hand, which is at the same level as his right hand and 0.60 m to the side. If the ball reaches a height of 0.80 m above the level of his hands, with what velocity does the ball leave his right hand?

8. A skateboarder is slowing down at a rate of 0.70 m/s². At the moment he is moving 1.5 m/s forward, he throws a basketball upward a distance of 3.0 m and catches it at the same level it was thrown without changing his position on the skateboard. Determine the vertical and horizontal components of the ball's velocity relative to the skateboard when the ball left his hand.

9. The beaters of an electric mixer are shown below.

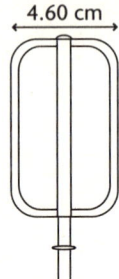

4.60 cm

What is the acceleration of the outer part of a blade as it rotates at a rate of 1200 revolutions per minute?

10. A clown rides a small car at a speed of 15 km/h along a circular path with a radius of 3.5 m.

   a. What is the magnitude of the centripetal force on a 0.18-kg ball held by the clown?

   b. At the point where the car is headed due north, the clown throws the ball vertically upward with a speed of 5.0 m/s relative to the moving car. To where must a second clown run to catch the ball the same distance above the ground as it was thrown?

8 Universal Gravitation

1. The satellites of Mars, Phobos and Deimos, have mean orbital radii of 9.38×10^6 m and 2.35×10^7 m, respectively. The orbital period of Deimos is 30.30 hr. Use Kepler's third law of planetary motion to predict the period of Phobos.

2. Use Kepler's third law to predict the altitude of a Martian satellite that would have a period of 24.0 h.

3. Use Newton's form of Kepler's third law and the information about Deimos in Problem 1 to determine the mass of Mars.

4. The Martian moon, *Deimos*, has a mass of 2.4×10^{15} kg and an average radius of 6.4 km. What is the acceleration of gravity at its surface?

5. What is the gravitational attraction between two protons ($m_{proton} = 1.67 \times 10^{-27}$ kg) at a distance of 5.0×10^{-15} m, about the diameter of the nucleus of an atom?

6. Two bowling balls, each with a mass of 6.80 kg, are 1.00 m apart. Compare the weight of the first ball with the gravitational force exerted on it by the second ball.

7. Saturn's rings are made of particles moving in orbits around the planet. The inner edge of the closest ring has a radius of 6.7×10^4 km while the radius of the outer edge of the farthest ring is 4.8×10^5 km. The mass of Saturn is 5.69×10^{26} kg.

   a. Calculate the velocity of a particle near the inner edge of the closest ring.

   b. What is the period of this particle?

   c. How do the answers of 6a and 6b compare to the velocity and period of a particle orbiting near the outer edge of the farthest ring?

8. The mass of the moon is 7.34×10^{22} kg and its average radius is 1785 km.

   a. Between January, 1998, and December, 1998, the *Lunar Prospector* was in a nearly circular orbit around the moon at an altitude of 1.0×10^2 km. What was the period of the *Lunar Prospector* in minutes?

   b. What was its velocity when it was in the orbit at 1.0×10^2 km?

9. At the moon's surface g_{Moon} has a value of 1.59 m/s². What is the value of the acceleration of gravity at an altitude of 1.00×10^2 km above the moon's surface?

10. Use Table 8-1 in the text to find the sun's gravitational field strength at Earth's orbit.

9 Momentum and Its Conservation

1. A 26.0-g arrow leaves a bowstring at a velocity of +46 m/s.

   a. What is the impulse on the arrow?

   b. What is the average force that the string exerts on the arrow if the string is in contact with the arrow for 6.0×10^{-3} s?

   c. What average force does the arrow exert on the string during this interval?

2. The *v-t* graph below shows the velocity changes of a 0.145-kg baseball as it is caught by player A and then by player B.

   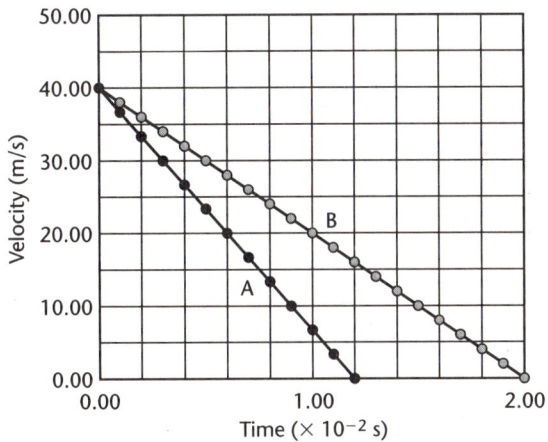

   a. Plot an *F-t* graph showing the impulse each player exerts on the ball.

   b. Explain which player more likely pulled back (moved in the direction of the ball) his glove while catching the ball.

3. After dropping from a height 1.50 m onto a concrete floor, a 50.0-g ball rebounds to a height of 0.90 m.

   a. Find the impulse acting on the ball as it dropped.

   b. Find the impulse acting on the ball on its rebound.

   c. Find the impulse on the ball while it was in contact with the floor.

4. A 180-kg crate is sitting on the flatbed of a moving truck. The coefficient of sliding friction between the crate and the truck bed is 0.30. Two taut cables are attached to either side of the crate. Each cable can exert a maximum horizontal force of 650 N either forward or backward if the crate begins to slide. If the truck stops in 1.8 s, what is the maximum speed the truck could have been moving without breaking the cables?

5. A single uranium atom has a mass of 3.97×10^{-25} kg. It decays into the nucleus of a thorium atom by emitting an alpha particle at a speed of 2.10×10^{7} m/s. The mass of an alpha particle is 6.68×10^{-27} kg. What is the recoil speed of the thorium nucleus?

6. A 62-kg boy on a 1.50-kg skateboard moving at +1.2 m/s steps off and lands on the sidewalk with a velocity of +1.1 m/s. How fast is the skateboard moving?

Physics: Principles and Problems *Supplemental Problems • Chapter 9*

9 Momentum and Its Conservation

7. A 60.0-kg girl with two 4.0-kg bricks is sitting on frictionless ice. She throws both bricks at the same time forward at a velocity of 6.00 m/s relative to her. What is the velocity of the girl?

8. The girl in Problem 7 throws one brick and then the other each with a velocity of 6.00 m/s relative to her. What is the velocity of the girl after she throws the second brick?

9. A boy and a dog are standing on a 110-kg diving raft in the middle of a lake. Just as the 55-kg boy dives off the raft with a horizontal velocity of 4.0 m/s due east, the 22-kg dog leaps off the raft horizontally with a velocity of 5.0 m/s due north. What is the resulting velocity of the raft?

10. A 2.00-kg puck moving to the right at a velocity of 6.00 m/s at an angle of 45.0° below the horizontal collides at point A with a 1.00-kg puck traveling to the right at a velocity of 3.00 m/s at an angle of 45.0° above the horizontal as shown below.

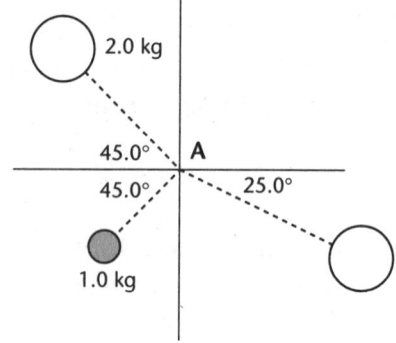

After the collision the 2.0-kg puck moves toward the right a velocity of 4.50 m/s at an angle of 25.0° below the horizontal. What is the velocity of the 1.0-kg puck immediately after the collision?

10 Energy, Work, and Simple Machines

1. A store manager places ten paint cans into a rectangle five cans long and two cans wide on the floor. He then tells an assistant to stack the remaining cans on the floor into a pyramidal display so that the second level is similar to the first. The third and fourth levels are each made up of eight cans arranged in a 4 × 2-can rectangle. The rest of the display should have every other remaining level decreasing by 2 cans. How much work does the assistant do in lifting the cans into position if each can weighs 46.0 N and is 0.20 m tall?

2. You exert a horizontal force of 4.6 N on a textbook sliding it 0.60 m across a library table to a friend.
   a. What amount of work do you do?
   b. You friend in Problem 2 returns the book by pushing it with a force of 6.2 N at an angle of 30.0 below the horizontal. What amount of work does your friend do?

3. A ski lift whisks a 75-kg skier at 3.0 m/s for 1.5 minutes along a cable that is inclined at an angle of 40.0° from the horizontal.
   a. How much work was done by the ski lift?
   b. How much power is expended by the ski lift?

4. An engine that has a power output 1.2 MW is used to propel an airplane that weighs 1.5×10^5 N. What is the maximum vertical speed that the plane can attain?

5. Armando expends 12 watts of power to maintain a horizontal swimming speed of 0.75 m/s.
   a. How much drag (resistance force) does the water exert on Armando?
   b. The drag on the swimmer is proportional to the square of the swimmer's speed. What power would Armando expend maintaining a swimming speed of 1.50 m/s?

6. A 40.0-N sack is attached to the wheel of a wheel-and-axle, which has a wheel-diameter of 30.00 cm and an axle-diameter of 6.00 cm.
   a. What is the *IMA* of the wheel-and-axle?
   b. If the effort force moves 0.40 m, what distance is the machine designed to lift the sack?

7. A 40.0-N sack is attached to the axle of the wheel-and-axle in Problem 6. Calculate the *IMA* and the distance the sack moves if the effort moves 0.40 m.

Physics: Principles and Problems

10 Energy, Work, and Simple Machines

8. Leah is helping to build a water habitat in a neighborhood park. The habitat includes an upper pond connected to a lower pond, 3.2 m below, by a trickling stream with several small cascades. At a home-building store, she finds a 45-W pump that has a maximum circulation rate of 1900 liters of water per hour. Determine if the pump is powerful enough to raise the water from the lower to upper pond? (The mass density of water, ρ, is 1.00 kg/L)

9. Using a block-and-tackle, a mover takes up 18.5 m of rope to raise a 115-kg stove from the ground to a window ledge 3.7 m high. What force must he exert on the rope if the efficiency of the block-and-tackle is 63%?

10. While unpacking a blind to hang, Rahul sees that the shaft of the blind, which rotates the horizontal slats, is connected to a small gearbox. The gearbox is also connected to the wand, which is turned to open and close the slats as shown below.

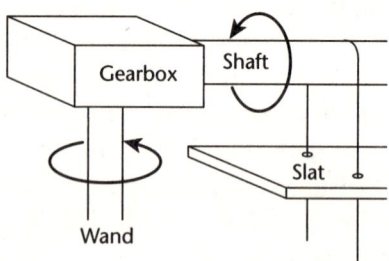

Rahul measures the wand's diameter as 1.00 cm and the shaft's diameter as 1.25 cm. He notes that to rotate the slats 180°, the wand has to make three complete rotations. Rahul concludes that the gearbox contains what ratio of the gear teeth?

11 Energy

1. Rae Ann weighs 530 N. What is her kinetic energy as she swims at a speed of 1.2 m/s?

2. In a hardware store, paint cans, which weigh 46 N each, are transported from storage to the back of the paint department by placing them on a 24°-ramp. The cans slide down the ramp at a constant speed of 3.4 m/s onto a table made of the same material as the ramp. How far does each can slide on the table?

3. Zeke begins to slide down a snow hill on a rubber mat. Zeke's mass is 76 kg and that of the mat is 2 kg.

   a. What is the change in the gravitational potential energy of Zeke and the mat when they are 1.2 m below the crest?

   b. Disregarding frictional forces, what is the change in the kinetic energy of Zeke and the mat when they are 1.2 m below the crest?

   c. Disregarding frictional forces, how fast are they moving when they are 1.2 m below the crest?

4. Kim is playing with a bead that slides on a wire as shown below.

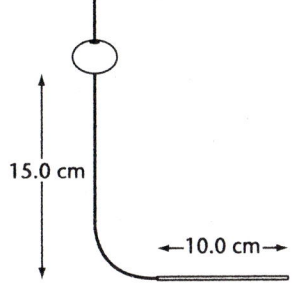

The wire and bead are frictionless but the white sheathing exerts a constant frictional force on the 5.0-g bead.

   a. When the bead is dropped as shown, it comes to rest 6.0 cm along the white sheathing. How much work does the white sheathing do on the bead?

   b. From what height should the bead be dropped so it stops at the end of the white sheathing?

6. Running at 4.0 m/s, Rafael grabs a vertical rope and swings upward. Assuming that air resistance is negligible, how far does Rafael rise?

7. A coiled spring gives a block of wood a kinetic energy of 1.50 J. The block slides up a ramp to a height that is 0.880 the height predicted using the conservation of mechanical energy.

   a. Plot graphs showing the gravitational potential energy and kinetic energy of the brick at the bottom of the incline and at the point where it comes to rest.

   b. How much mechanical energy was lost?

8. Erin raises the 1.20-kg bob of a pendulum to a level at which its gravitational potential energy is 3.00 J.

   a. Predict the speed of the bob as it passes through its lowest point.

11 Energy

b. Erin releases the bob from rest and uses a photogate to measure its speed as it passes through its lowest point. She finds that the speed is 93.2% of the predicted value. How much work did frictional forces do on the pendulum?

c. The pendulum's original energy was decreased by what percentage due to the work done by frictional forces on the pendulum as it moved from its release point through its lowest point?

9. Steve can consistently throw a 0.200-kg ball at a speed of 12.0 m/s. On one throw the ball passes the top of a flagpole, which is 6.00 m above the ball's initial position.

    a. What is the ball's gravitational potential energy when it passes the top of the flagpole? (Assume the ball's initial gravitational energy is 0 J).

    b. What is the ball's kinetic energy as it passes the top of the flagpole?

    c. Steve throws the ball straight upward. What is the ball's velocity as it first passes the top of the flagpole?

    d. Steve throws the ball at a speed of 12.0 m/s so that it just reaches the top of the flagpole. What is the ball's velocity at the top of the flagpole?

    e. For question 9 d, what is the ball's initial velocity?

10. A skateboarding area has two ramps. The first ramp has a height of 0.30 m and the second a height of 0.60 m. A 2.0-kg skateboard is released from rest at the top of the first ramp and rolls down the ramp onto the level ground. There a 47-kg skateboarder jumps on it and rides it up the second ramp. With what horizontal velocity must the skateboarder mount the skateboard as it moves on the level so that the board just reaches the top of the second ramp? (Assume that frictional forces on the skateboard wheels are negligible.)

12 Thermal Energy

1. The freezing point of bromine −7.25°C. Its boiling point is 59.35°C.

   What is the state of bromine at the following temperatures?

   a. 251 K

   b. 305 K

   c. 342 K

2. Octane, a substance found in petroleum, boils at 126°C and is a liquid over a range of 183 Celsius degrees. What is the melting point of octane in kelvins?

3. How much energy is required to heat a clay pizza baking stone, which has a specific heat of 860 J/kg·K, from 25°C to 235°C? The mass of the stone is 4.8 kg.

4. A 2.0-kg slab of concrete requires 11 kJ to raise its temperature from 23°C to 29°C. What is the specific heat of concrete?

5. A blacksmith lifts a 0.73-kg iron horseshoe from a forge at a temperature of 835°C and quenches the shoe in 45 kg of water at 23°C. What is the final temperature of the horseshoe and water?

6. A silversmith pours 55.0 g of molten silver at 975°C into a mold and lets it cool to 25°C. How much heat does the silver transfer to the environment? The melting point of silver is 961°C and the specific heat of molten silver is 288 J/kg·K.

7. Angie adds a block of ice at −4°C to cool 2.2 kg of water at 42°C in an insulated jug. When the water has cooled to 5°C, she removes the remaining ice. What is the mass of water in the jug?

8. A cubic meter of water in a perfectly insulated container is exposed to solar energy during a 24-hour period as shown below.

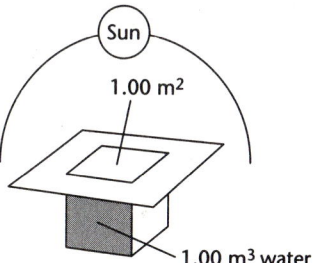

   At the end of the 24 hours, the temperature of the water increases by 0.60°C. If all the solar energy was absorbed by the water though a 1.00 m² surface, what is the daily solar energy intensity measured in J/m²? (The density of water is 1.00×10^3 kg/m³.)

13 States of Matter

1. Marcos sets a can of paint, which weighs 46 N, on a shelf. The bottom of the paint can has a small lip on the which the can sits. The outer diameter of the lip is 16.8 cm and has a width of 2 mm. What pressure does the lip exert on the shelf?

2. During a 12-h period, the atmospheric pressure varied from 98 kPa to 105 kPa. By how much did the force acting on a 1.0-cm^2 patch of your skin vary?

3. With its full compliment of passengers, crew, and cargo, the *RMS Titanic* is reported to have a displacement of about 4.7×10^3 m^3 of water. What was the ship's weight?

4. A spherical balloon, filled with helium, is tethered to the ground by a string. If the tension in the string is 7.5 N, what is the volume of the balloon? (Ignore the mass of the balloon.) The mass densities of air and helium are 1.2 kg/m^3 and 0.177 kg/m^3, respectively.

5. Exploring an ancient shipwreck off the coast of Greece, an underwater archeologist is in a submersible that reaches a depth of 3.00 km.
   a. What is the external pressure on the submersible if the density of seawater is 1.04×10^3 kg/m^3 at this depth?
   b. If the interior of the submersible is maintained at a pressure of 101 kPa, what force acts on a porthole that has a diameter of 10.0 cm?

6. What does a coffee mug, which has a volume of 8×10^{-5} m^3 and weighs 3.3 N in air, weigh submerged in a sink full of water?

7. On a lakeshore, Leon finds a log that has a diameter of 0.16 m and a length of 2.0 m. He rolls the log, weighing 280 N, into the lake. What is the maximum weight the floating log can carry without submerging?

8. In a foundry a worker heats a 27-cm long iron spike from 20°C to a temperature of 950°C in a forge. By how much has the length of the spike increased?

9. A helium-filled balloon, which has an initial volume of 8.0 m^3 at 28°C, is placed in a hangar at an airport. Overnight the interior temperature of the hangar falls from 28°C to 13°C. What is the volume of the balloon the next morning?

10. What buoyancy was lost overnight by the helium-filled balloon in Problem 9? Assume the density of air is 1.2 kg/m^3.

Physics: Principles and Problems

14 Waves and Energy Transfer

1. Sonya hears water dripping from the eaves of the house onto a porch roof. She counts 20 drops in one minute.
   a. What is the period of the drops?
   b. What is the frequency of the drops?

2. You scrape a long nail across a metal file. The speed of the nail is 25 cm/s and the file has groves that are 1.0 mm apart. What is the frequency of the "clicks" made by the nail?

3. Hiroshi is generating waves on a rope by flipping the rope up and down. Each motion up or down lasts 0.20 s. The distance from a crest to a trough is 0.40 m.
   a. What is the amplitude of the wave?
   b. What is the frequency of the waves?

4. Ripples in a pond each have a wavelength of 8.0 cm and frequency of 3.0 Hz. What is the speed of a ripple?

5. A Love wave, one of the four types of waves associated with earthquakes, is a transverse wave in which the surface of the earth moves back and forth as the wave passes. What is the period of a Love wave that has speed of 4.1 km/s and a wavelength of 620 km?

6. Two pulses, one with a length of 0.30 m and an amplitude of 0.24 m and the other with a length of 0.54 m and an amplitude of −0.13 m, approach each other on a rope.
   a. What is the amplitude of the rope at the point where the midpoints of the pulses pass each other?
   b. What is the pulse length when the midpoints of the pulses pass each other?

7. Figure 14-1a shows a pulse traveling at a speed of 1.0 m/s in a coiled spring to which a second spring is attached at point A. Figure 14-1b shows the springs a few moments later.

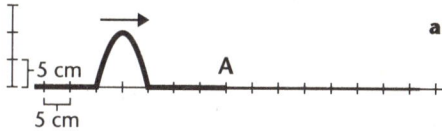

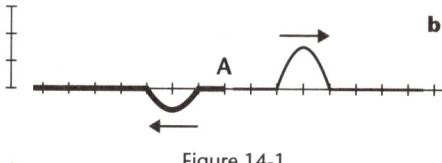

Figure 14-1

   a. What is the amplitude of the incident pulse?
   b. What is the speed of the reflected pulse?
   c. What is the speed of the transmitted pulse?

14 Waves and Energy Transfer

8. In Figure 14-2 a pulse is traveling at a speed of 1.0 m/s in a coiled spring to which a second spring is attached at point A. Figure 14-2b shows the location of the transmitted pulse, which has a speed of 0.80 m/s.

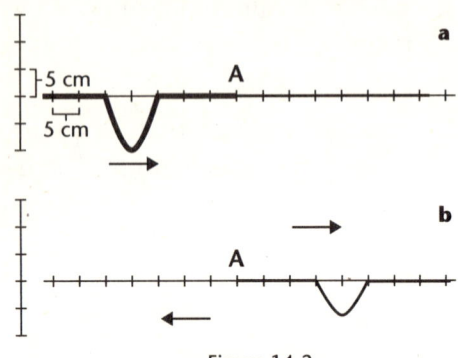

Figure 14-2

   a. What is the speed of the reflected pulse?
   b. Is the reflected pulse erect or inverted?

9. A physics teacher attaches an electric oscillator to one end of a 2.0-m long, horizontal spring and attaches the other end to a stationary hook in a wall. She adjusts the frequency of the oscillator to produce a standing wave in the spring. Students observe that the standing wave has 3 nodes and 2 antinodes. She then doubles the frequency of the oscillations and produces another standing wave. How many nodes and antinodes do the students observe in the standing wave?

10. A water wave with a wavelength of 7.0 cm and speed of 21 cm/s moves into a more shallow part of a pond where its wavelength is 6.0 cm.

   a. What is the frequency of the wave on the shallow water?
   b. What is the velocity of the wave in the more shallow water?

15 Sound

Assume the speed of sound in air is 343 m/s unless otherwise noted.

1. Animal behavior researchers hypothesize that elephants communicate by producing and detecting low-pitched sounds. The sound waves of one such sound have a frequency of 150 Hz. What is the wavelength of the sound wave?

2. Wayne is swimming underwater in a lake when a large rock falls from a ledge into the lake. If Wayne is 75 m from the place where the rock enters the water, at what time later will Wayne hear the splash? The speed of sound is 1460 m/s in cool lake water.

For questions 3–5 use the following information.
The equation for the Doppler shift of a wave of speed v reaching a moving detector is

$$f_d = f_s \frac{(v + v_d)}{(v - v_s)}$$

where v_d is the speed of the detector, v_s is the speed of the source, f_s is the frequency of the source, and f_d is the frequency of the detector. If the detector moves toward the source, v_d is positive, if the source moves toward the detector, v_s is positive.

3. While fishing off a boat anchored offshore, you note that the distance between successive wave crests is about 12 m and their speed is about 7.5 m/s.
    a. What is the frequency of the waves?
    b. If the boat hoists anchor and heads out to sea at a speed of 15 m/s, what will you observe as the wave frequency?

4. On board a fishing boat heading out to sea at a speed of 15 m/s, another fishing boat behind you sounds a 510-Hz horn as it heads toward the shore at a speed 18 m/s. What is the frequency of the sound waves from the horn that reach you?

5. A species of bat navigates by emitting short bursts of sound waves that have a frequency range that peaks at 58.0 kHz.
    a. If the bat is flying at 4.0 m/s toward a stationary object, what is the frequency of the sound waves reaching the object?
    b. What is the frequency of the reflected sound waves detected by the bat?
    c. What is the difference between the frequency of the sound waves emitted by the bat and the frequency of the sound waves detected by the bat if the bat is flying at 4.0 m/s and the object is a moth approaching at 1.0 m/s?

6. A monitor detects the pressure amplitude of the sound wave from a thunderclap as 6×10^{-1} Pa and displays the sound level as 90 dB. A second more distant monitor displays the sound level of the thunderclap as 70 dB. What pressure amplitude did the second monitor detect?

7. The strings of a standard guitar are tuned to the following frequencies: 165, 220, 294, 392, 494, and 659 Hz.
    a. Find the lengths of open-ended organ pipes that would produce the same frequencies.
    b. Sketch the pipes showing their lengths to scale.

15 Sound

8. Carla takes a 22.0-cm length of rigid, plastic tubing and places it into a glass of water so that one end of the tube is submerged 3.0 cm. She gently blows across the opposite end of the tube. What frequency sound waves will the tube produce?

9. The fundamental tone of an open-pipe resonator with a length of 0.22 m is the same as the first harmonic of a closed-pipe resonator. What is the length of the closed-pipe resonator?

10. You receive a cassette tape with the following note. "The first sound on the tape is the sound of a 442-Hz tuning fork and a second tuning fork being struck simultaneously. The second sound on the tape is the sound of the second tuning fork and a 444-Hz tuning fork being struck simultaneously. What is the frequency of the second tuning fork?" Listening to the tape you hear that the first sound has a beat frequency of 3 Hz and the second sound has beat frequency of 5 Hz. Answer the question found in the note.

16 Light

1. Calculate the frequency of violet light, $\lambda = 434$ nm.

2. Calculate the wavelength of infrared radiation, $f = 2.66 \times 10^{13}$ Hz, as it travels through a vacuum.

3. When Mars and Earth are closest together in their orbits, they are about 5.4×10^7 km apart. When the two planets are most distant from each other, they are about 4.01×10^8 km apart. How much more time would it take for an astronomer on Earth to observe an event on Mars when the two planets are farthest apart compared to when the planets are closest together? Use the speed of light in a vacuum.

4. A 90-watt halogen "energy-saving" incandescent bulb has a light output of 1780 lm. What illumination will this bulb provide on a surface 39 cm from the bulb?

5. What is the luminous flux of an incandescent bulb that provides illumination of 84.5 lx at a distance of 1.32 m from the bulb?

6. Calculate the candle power of an incandescent bulb that provides 1580 lm of luminous flux.

7. Calculate the candle power of a point source of light that provides 1330 lx of illumination at a distance of 8.00 m.

8. What illumination does the light source in problem 7 provide at a distance of 2.00 m?

9. What wavelengths of visible light are reinforced when white light is reflected from a soap film 176 nm thick?

17 Reflection and Refraction

1. A ray of light in air strikes the surface of a liquid at an angle of 65° with the normal. The refracted ray is at an angle of 42° with the normal. What is the index of refraction of this liquid?

2. Lead(II) oxide is commonly added to glass to increase its index of refraction. A typical leaded glass has an index of refraction of 1.81. What is the angle of refraction of a light ray in air that is incident on this type of glass at an angle of 32.5°?

3. A layer of the solvent toluene is floating on water in a glass container. A ray of light passing through the water is incident upon the toluene layer at an angle of 58.3°. The angle of the refracted beam in the toluene is 49.0°. Calculate the index of refraction of toluene.

4. A ray of light passing through water enters a different material at an incident angle of 27.4° and is refracted so that the angle of refraction is 31.5°. Is the speed of light in the material faster or slower than the speed of light in water? Explain your answer and show your reasoning in mathematical form.

5. The index of refraction of the polycarbonate plastic from which CDs and DVDs are made is 1.55. What is the speed of light as it passes through the plastic?

6. A certain ray of green light has a wavelength of 5.40×10^{-7} m in air. What is the wavelength of this light as it passes through a diamond, $n_{diamond}$ = 2.42? Consider how the frequency (color) of the light is affected as it travels in the diamond.

7. What is the critical angle for a light ray passing into air from polystyrene plastic, $n_{polystyrene}$ = 1.60?

8. The critical angle of a material is 45.0°. What is the index of refraction of this material?

Physics: Principles and Problems

18 Mirrors and Lenses

1. A student views an image of a vase in a plane mirror. The apparent height of the vase's image is 32 cm and the image appears 45 cm behind the mirror. How tall is the actual vase and how far in front of the mirror is the vase?

2. A student uses a spherical concave mirror to focus the sun's rays to start a campfire. The sunlight comes to a focus 12.6 cm from the center of the mirror. What is the mirror's radius of curvature?

3. What is the focal length of a spherical, concave mirror that has a radius of curvature of 426 mm?

4. A spotlight has a spherical, concave mirror acting as a reflector. Its radius of curvature is 2.26 m. Where should a bulb be placed so that the mirror reflects a straight beam of parallel rays? Describe the beam that would be produced by the spotlight if the bulb is placed closer to the mirror?

5. A spherical, concave mirror has a radius of curvature of 85.6 cm. A candle is placed on the principal axis 91.0 cm from the center of the mirror. At what distance from the mirror will a real image of the candle form?

6. A flower is placed in front of a concave, spherical mirror at a distance of 0.350 m from the center of the mirror. A real image of the flower is observed at a distance of 0.288 m from the center of the mirror. Calculate the focal length of the mirror.

7. If the flower in problem 6 is 8.7 cm tall, how tall is the image of the flower?

8. Most U.S. passenger cars manufactured in recent years have slightly convex side mirrors on the right side. Suppose your car is equipped with a convex mirror that has a radius of curvature of 7.24 m. How far away will a following car appear to be if it is actually 15.5 m away?

9. A convex lens with a focal length of 16.6 cm is used to form a real image of an object placed 35.0 cm from the lens. The height of the object is 4.5 cm. Calculate the size and distance of the real image that is formed.

10. The lens of a certain movie projector has a focal length of 22.50 cm. When a frame of film is in place, it is 23.25 cm from the lens. At what distance from the lens would you place a screen in order to receive a focused image? If the image on the film is 28 mm high, how tall is the image formed on the screen?

11. Since 1838, the diameter of dimes minted in the United States has been standardized at 17.9 mm. A magnifying lens that has a 125-mm focal length is used to view a dime. If the dime is placed 52.5 mm from the lens, what is the size and distance of the virtual image?

12. The lens of a magnifying loupe forms a 30.0-mm image of a 2.2 mm insect when the insect is placed 25 mm from the lens. What is the focal length of this lens?

13. A student views a tree that is 27.5 m tall through a concave lens that has a focal length of −70.0 cm. If the tree is 34.0 m away, how tall is the virtual image of the tree?

19 Diffraction and Interference of Light

1. Green light of a certain wavelength is incident upon two slits separated by 2.10×10^{-5} m. A screen is placed 0.800 m from the slits. The distance from the central bright line to the first-order line is 19.9 mm. What is the wavelength of the light?

2. A double-slit grating must be calibrated before use. A laser diode emitting light of wavelength 668.2 nm is shined on the slits. On a screen placed 1.000 m away, the first-order line appears 34.3 mm from the central bright line. What is the distance between the slits of the grating?

3. Light from a He-Ne laser (λ = 632.8 nm) strikes a single slit and is diffracted. On a screen placed 0.850 m away, the first dark band appears at a distance of 10.6 mm from the central bright line. What is the width of the slit?

4. Monochromatic blue light of unknown wavelength shines on a slit that is 0.052 mm wide. On a screen placed 1.15 m from the slit, the first dark band appears at a distance of 10.1 mm from the central bright line. Calculate the wavelength of the light.

5. A spectrometer has a grating in which lines are 1.50×10^{-6} m apart. If monochromatic red light having wavelength of 668 nm is shined on the grating, at what angle will the first-order bright line appear?

6. A certain spectroscope uses a grating having 1.00×10^4 lines/cm. What wavelength of light will produce a first-order bright line at an angle of 37.5° from the axis?

7. A certain spectroscope produces a first-order line at an angle of 42.9° when 668-nm light from a He-Ne laser is used. What is the distance between the lines of the grating?

8. Light from a hydrogen discharge tube is shined through a grating that has a line density of 8550 lines/cm. At what angles from the center axis would you expect to find the 486-nm and the 656-nm lines of the hydrogen emission spectrum?

9. Light from the strong yellow (λ = 589 nm) emission line of a sodium vapor lamp is shined through a diffraction grating that has a distance of 1.04×10^{-6} m between slits. A screen stands 1.20 m from the grating. At what distance from the center bright line will the first-order bright line appear?

20 Static Electricity

1. How many excess electrons are on a sphere with a charge of -9.20×10^{-17} C?

2. Two charges, q_1 and q_2, are separated by a distance, d, and exert a force, F, on each other. Identify what new force will exist if
   a. q_1 is doubled and q_2 is cut in half.
   b. q_1 is tripled and q_2 is doubled.
   c. q_2 is cut in half and d is tripled.

3. An electric force of 0.030 N acts between two charges which are 7.2 cm apart. Calculate the force acting between the charges if the distance between them is reduced to 1.5 cm.

4. Two negative charges of -24 µC each are separated by 6.0 cm. What force exists between the charges?

5. Two charged spheres are separated by 315 mm. What is the force between them if the charge on one sphere is $+9.6 \times 10^{-7}$ C and the charge on the other sphere is -2.2×10^{-5} C?

6. Determine the electrostatic force of attraction between a proton and an electron that are separated by 7.5×10^{-8} m.

7. A positive charge of 3.4×10^{-7} C exerts a repulsive force of 9.0 N on a second charge 4.0 cm away. Determine the second charge.

8. An attractive force of 0.87 N exists between a positive charge of 5.0 µC and a negative charge of -1.5 µC. What is the distance between the charges?

9. Two identical point charges exert a repulsive force of 6.0×10^{-3} N when separated by a distance of 6.5 cm. Calculate the charge of each.

10. Two positively charged spheres, A and B, are separated by 0.25 m. The charge on sphere A is one third the charge on sphere B. Find the charge on each sphere if the force of repulsion is 125 N.

11. Three particles are placed in a straight line. The left particle has a charge of $+2.0 \times 10^{-5}$ C, the middle particle has a charge of -4.0×10^{-6} C, and the right particle has a charge of $+3.0 \times 10^{-5}$ C. The left particle is 56 mm from the middle particle and the right particle is 42 mm from the middle particle. Find the net force on the left particle.

12. A positive charge of 23 µC is 15 cm directly north of a positive charge of 38 µC. A third positive charge of 71 µC is 45 cm directly west of the 38-µC charge. Determine the net force on the 38-µC charge.

Physics: Principles and Problems

Supplemental Problems • Chapter 20

21 Electric Fields

1. A positive test charge of 3.0 μC experiences a force of 0.75 N in an electric field. What is the magnitude of the electric field at the location of the test charge?

2. A negative charge of 9.0×10^{-7} C experiences a force of 0.028 N to the left in an electric field. What are the field magnitude and direction?

3. A charge of 4.00 μC is placed in an electric field of intensity 6.50×10^5 N/C. What is the size of the force on the charge?

4. An electric field with an intensity of 1.5×10^4 N/C exerts a force of 8.1×10^{-3} N on a positive charge. What is the magnitude of the charge?

5. Two large, charged parallel plates are 25 cm apart. The magnitude of the electric field between the plates is 1.6×10^3 N/C. What is the electric potential difference between the plates?

6. A voltmeter reads 412 V across two charged parallel plates that are 125 mm apart. What is the electric field between them?

7. The potential difference between two charged parallel plates is 720 V. What is the distance between the plates if the electric field between them is 2.4×10^4 N/C?

8. How much work is required to move a charge of 5.5×10^{-8} C between two points that have a potential difference of 92.5 V?

9. When a charge of 8.50 mC is moved between two points in an electric field, 3.72 J of work are performed. What is the potential difference between the two points?

10. A positively charged oil drop weighs 2.7×10^{-13} N. It is suspended in an electric field of 4.2×10^5 N/C.
    a. What is the charge on the drop?
    b. How many electrons is the drop missing?

11. How strong is the electric field that will suspend an oil drop that carries two excess electrons and weighs 6.9×10^{-15} N?

12. An oil drop carrying seven excess electrons is suspended between two charged parallel plates. The plates are separated by a distance of 2.0 cm, and there is a potential difference of 950 V between the plates.
    a. What is the sign of the charge on the lower plate?
    b. What is the weight of the suspended oil drop?

13. A capacitor with a charge of 0.40 mC has an electric potential difference of 19 V across it. What is the capacitance of the capacitor?

14. A 120-pF capacitor is connected across a 7500-V potential difference. What is the charge on the capacitor?

15. What is the voltage across a capacitor with a charge of 8.0×10^{-5} C and a capacitance of 3.0 mF?

16. Both capacitor A and capacitor B have the same charge, but the voltage across capacitor A is 12 V while the voltage across capacitor B is 54 V. Compare the capacitances of the two capacitors.

22 Current Electricity

1. The current through a lamp is 2.50 A.
   a. How many coulombs of charge pass through the lamp in 4.00 min?
   b. How many electrons pass through the lamp in 4.00 min?

2. What power is supplied to a digital clock that operates on a 120-V line and draws 0.0375 A of current?

3. A hair dryer uses 680 W of power while connected to a 120-V outlet. What is the current through the hair dryer?

4. A flashlight uses two 1.5-V batteries. The current through the flashlight bulb is 1.2 A.
   a. How much power does the flashlight use?
   b. How much electric energy is converted when the flashlight is operated for 45 s?

5. A resistor is connected to a 9.0-V battery. What is the resistance of the resistor if the current in the circuit is 0.73 A?

6. A lamp with a resistance of 576 Ω is connected to a 120-V source.
   a. What is the current through the lamp?
   b. What is the power rating of the lamp?

7. When a 62-Ω resistor is connected to a battery, the current in the circuit is 0.39 A. What is the voltage of the battery?

8. A television is rated at 275 W and operates on a 120-V outlet.
   a. What is the current through the television?
   b. What is the resistance of the television?

9. Draw a series-circuit diagram including a 75.0-V battery, an ammeter that reads 833 mA, and a resistor. Label the size of the resistor and indicate the direction of current.

10. A current of 4.6 A is measured through a 7.8-Ω resistor for 1.75 min. How much heat is generated by the resistor?

11. A 15-W fluorescent lightbulb draws a current of 0.125 A. What is the resistance of the lightbulb?

12. A 267-Ω resistor is connected to a 45.0-V battery. How much thermal energy is produced by the resistor in 3.5 min?

13. What is the current through a 2250-W electric heater that has an operating resistance of 6.4 Ω?

14. A computer monitor uses 85 W and is in use 4.0 hours per day. At 11¢ per kWh, what is the cost of operating the monitor for 30 days?

15. A CD player draws 0.29 A from a 120-V source.
   a. How much power does the CD player use?
   b. If the CD player is operated for an average of 2.5 hours per day, how much energy in kWh does it consume in one year?

16. An electric fan with a resistance of 261 Ω is connected to a 120-V source.
   a. How much current does it draw?
   b. How much power does it use?
   c. At 12.5¢ per kWh, how much does it cost to operate the fan for 12 hours?

17. A 17.0-W compact fluorescent lamp provides as much light as a 60.0-W incandescent lightbulb.
   a. At 11¢ per kWh, what is the cost of operating the compact fluorescent lamp over its lifetime of 1.0×10^4 hours?
   b. At 11¢ per kWh, what is the cost of operating a 60.0-W lightbulb for 1.0×10^4 hours?

23 Series and Parallel Circuits

1. Three 25.0-Ω resistors are connected in series across a 60.0-V battery.
   a. What is the equivalent resistance of the circuit?
   b. What is the current in the circuit?
   c. What is the voltage drop across each resistor?

2. A string of 36 identical holiday lights is connected in series to a 120-V source. The current through the bulbs is 0.40 A.
   a. What is the equivalent resistance of the light string?
   b. What is the resistance of each bulb?
   c. What power is dissipated by the light string?

3. A lamp with a resistance of 8 Ω is connected across a 24-V battery.
   a. What is the current through the lamp?
   b. What resistance must be connected in series with the lamp to reduce the current to 1.6 A?

4. A 12-Ω resistor and a 28-Ω resistor are connected in series across a battery. The current in the circuit is 0.90 A.
   a. What is the voltage of the battery?
   b. What is the voltage drop across the 12-W resistor?

5. Three resistors are connected in series across a 75-V potential difference. R_1 is 170 Ω and R_2 is 190 Ω. The potential difference across R_3 is 21 V.
   a. Find the current in the circuit.
   b. Find the resistance of R_3.

6. A 15-V battery and two resistors, R_B of 36 Ω and R_A of 84 Ω, are connected as a voltage divider. What is the voltage across the 36-W resistor?

7. Maria is designing a voltage divider using a 30.0-V battery and a 375-Ω resistor as R_B. What resistor should be used as R_A if the output voltage across R_B is to be 22.5 V?

8. A 25-Ω resistor, a 55-Ω resistor, and a 75-Ω resistor are connected in parallel and placed across a 9.0-V battery.
   a. What is the equivalent resistance of the parallel circuit?
   b. What is the current through the entire circuit?
   c. What is the current through each branch of the circuit?

9. Suppose that the 25-Ω resistor in problem 8 is replaced by a 45-Ω resistor. Without performing any calculations, describe qualitatively the change in each of the following.
   a. the equivalent resistance of the parallel circuit
   b. the current through the entire circuit
   c. the current through each branch of the circuit

Physics: Principles and Problems

23 Series and Parallel Circuits

10. Two resistors, one 130 Ω and the other 210 Ω, are connected in parallel. The resistors are then connected to a battery. If the current through the entire circuit is 0.31 A, what is the voltage of the battery?

11. Resistors R_1, R_2, and R_3 are connected in parallel. R_1 is 68 Ω and R_2 is 93 Ω. The equivalent resistance of the parallel combination is 26 Ω. What is the resistance of R_3?

12. Four identical resistors are connected in parallel. The equivalent resistance of the parallel combination is 4.5 Ω. What is the resistance of each resistor?

13. A 120-V household circuit that contains a 320-W television, a 1.0×10^2-W lamp, and a 1350-W heater is connected to a 2.0×10^1-A fuse. Will the fuse melt if all three devices are operating simultaneously? Explain.

14. Resistors R_1, R_2, and R_3 have resistances of 37.0 Ω, 22.0 Ω, and 41.0 Ω respectively. R_1 and R_2 are connected in series, and their combination is in parallel with R_3. This arrangement is then placed across a 60.0-V battery.
  a. Draw the circuit diagram.
  b. What is the equivalent resistance of the three resistors?
  c. What is the current in the circuit?
  d. What is the current through R_3?
  e.. What is the potential difference across R_1?

15. A 19-Ω resistor is connected in series to a 45-V battery and two 12-Ω resistors that are connected in parallel to each other.
  a. Draw the circuit diagram.
  b. What is the equivalent resistance of the three resistors?
  c. What is the current in the circuit?
  d. What is the current through one of the 12-Ω resistors?
  e. What is the potential difference across the 19-Ω resistor?

24 Magnetic Fields

1. How does the strength of the magnetic field around a wire change if the current in the wire is increased from 0.25 A to 1.75 A?

2. What is the direction of the force on a current-carrying wire in a magnetic field if the current is toward the right on a page and the magnetic field is out of the page?

3. A wire 0.80 m long carrying a current of 3.2 A is perpendicular to a 0.15-T magnetic field. What is the force on the wire?

4. A wire 375 cm long is perpendicular to Earth's magnetic field. Calculate the force on the wire if the current in the wire is 16 A.

5. The force on a 0.65 m wire at right angles to a uniform magnetic field is 8.3×10^{-2} N. The current in the wire is 2.1 A. What is the strength of the magnetic field?

6. A wire 7.0 m long is perpendicular to a 2.6-T magnetic field. A 9.5-N force acts on the wire. What is the current in the wire?

7. A galvanometer has a full-scale deflection when the current is 100.0 µA. If the galvanometer has a resistance of 1.0 kΩ, what should be the resistance of the series (multiplier) resistor to make a voltmeter with a full-scale deflection of 5.0 V?

8. A beam of electrons moves from the back to the front of a room. The beam is deflected rightward, when facing the back of the room, by a magnetic field. What is the direction of the field causing the deflection?

9. A beam of protons travels at right angles to a magnetic field of 4.0×10^{-2} T. The protons have a speed of 5.3×10^6 m/s. What is the size of the force on each proton?

10. Doubly ionized particles in a beam carry a net positive charge of two elementary charge units. The beam moves at a velocity of 6.1×10^4 m/s perpendicular to a magnetic field of 0.35 T. What is the magnitude of the force acting on each particle?

11. An electron is traveling at 1.4×10^7 m/s at right angles to a magnetic field. The electron experiences a force of 4.7×10^{-13} N. How strong is the magnetic field?

12. A doubly ionized particle experiences a force of 9.2×10^{-14} N when it travels at right angles through a 1.8-T magnetic field. What is the speed of the particle?

13. A magnetic field of 0.50 T acts in a direction due north. An unknown particle travels due east through the field at 8.7×10^5 m/s. The particle experiences an upward force of 2.1×10^{-13} N.
    a. Does the particle carry a net positive charge or a net negative charge?
    b. How many elementary charges does the particle carry?

Physics: Principles and Problems

25 Electromagnetic Induction

1. An east-west wire is moved toward the south through a magnetic field that is pointing up, out of Earth. What is the direction of the induced current?

2. A straight wire, 1.8 m long, moves at 5.0 m/s perpendicular to a magnetic field of strength 6.0×10^{-2} T.
   a. What *EMF* is induced in the wire?
   b. The wire is part of a circuit that has a total resistance of 1.2 Ω. What is the current through the wire?

3. A straight wire, 85 cm long, is moved straight up at a speed of 14 m/s through a 0.70-T magnetic field pointed horizontally.
   a. What *EMF* is induced in the wire?
   b. The wire is part of a circuit with a total resistance of 3.0 Ω. What is the current in the circuit?

4. An *EMF* of 0.46 V is induced in a wire 2.5 m long when it is moving perpendicularly across a uniform magnetic field at a speed of 2.0 m/s. What is the strength of the magnetic field?

5. At what speed would a 35-cm length of wire have to move at right angles to a 1.0-T magnetic field to induce an *EMF* of 1.5 V?

6. The direction of a 2.8-T magnetic field is northward, 30° above the horizontal. An east-west wire, 4.0 m long, moves horizontally northward at a speed of 1.25 m/s.
   a. What is the vertical component of the magnetic field?
   b. What *EMF* is induced in the wire?

7. An AC generator develops a maximum voltage of 315 V.
   a. What is the effective voltage in a circuit placed across the generator?
   b. The resistance of the circuit is 66 Ω. What is the effective current?

8. The effective voltage of an AC household outlet is 120 V. The effective current through a lamp connected to the outlet is 0.29 A.
   a. What is the maximum current through the lamp?
   b. What is the peak power dissipated by the lamp?

9. A fuse in a 120-V household circuit will melt if the instantaneous current reaches 25.5 A.
   a. What is the largest effective current that the fuse will allow?
   b. What is the largest effective power dissipation that the fuse will allow?

10. A step-up transformer has 60 turns on its primary coil and 4500 turns on its secondary coil. The primary circuit is supplied with an effective AC voltage of 240 V.
    a. What is the voltage in the secondary circuit?
    b. The current in the secondary circuit is 0.36 A. What is the current in the primary circuit?
    c. What power is drawn by the primary circuit? What power is supplied by the secondary circuit?

11. The primary coil of a transformer has 90 turns. It is connected to a 120-V AC source. Calculate the number of turns on the secondary coil needed to supply these voltages.
    a. 8.0 V
    b. 44 V
    c. 7600 V

12. A 5.0-kW transformer has an input voltage of 1250 V and an output current of 56 A.
    a. What is the ratio of turns on the secondary coil to turns on the primary coil?
    b. Is this a step-up or step-down transformer?

Physics: Principles and Problems   *Supplemental Problems • Chapter 25*

26 Electromagnetism

1. A beam of electrons travels an undeflected path in a Thomson tube. $E = 8.0 \times 10^3$ N/C. $B = 4.5 \times 10^{-2}$ T. What is the speed of the electrons as they travel through the tube?

2. An electron moving at 2.0×10^6 m/s moves through a magnetic field of 8.0×10^{-2} T. What is the radius of the electron's path. The mass of an electron is 9.11×10^{-31} kg. $q = 1.6 \times 10^{-19}$.

3. A magnetic field and an electric field are perpendicular to each other in a Thomson tube. The electric field intensity is 5.0×10^4 N/C, and the intensity of the magnetic field is 3.0×10^{-2} T. What is the speed of the moving particles?

4. A charged particle is accelerated from rest through a potential difference of 8.0×10^2 V. It enters a magnetic field of 5.0×10^{-2} T. The radius of curvature is 6.0×10^{-2} m.
   a. Calculate the m/q ratio.
   b. If the particle has a charge of 1.6×10^{-19} C, what is its mass?

5. Alpha particles are accelerated through a potential difference of 8.0×10^2 V. The particles have a mass of 6.68×10^{-27} kg and a charge of twice that of an electron. If the magnetic field is 0.30 T, what is the radius of the path of the particles?

6. A proton moves with the speed of 9.0×10^3 m/s through a magnetic field of 4.5×10^{-2} T. The charge on the proton is equal to the charge on the electron only positive. The mass of the proton is 1.67×10^{-27} kg. What is the radius of the circular path?

7. A beam of electrons is bent in a circular path with a radius of 3.0 cm by a magnetic field of 5.0×10^{-4} T. What is the speed of the electrons?

8. A proton moves across a 3.0-T magnetic field. The radius of curvature of the path is 1.5×10^{-2} m.
   a. What is the speed of the proton?
   b. The proton follows a straight line when an electric field is applied at right angles to the magnetic field. What is the strength of the electric field?

9. A lithium ion with a speed of 7.0×10^5 m/s and a charge of 1.6×10^{-19} C enters the magnetic field of a mass spectrometer. The magnetic field is 0.28 T, and the radius of the ion path is 0.30 m. Find the mass of the lithium ion.

10. An electron and a proton move at the same speed as they enter a 3.0×10^{-2} T magnetic field. The electron moves in a circular path of radius 8.0×10^{-3} m. Calculate the radius of the path of the proton.

Physics: Principles and Problems

26 Electromagnetism

11. A mass spectrometer produces a beam of doubly ionized calcium ions. They are first accelerated by a potential difference of 82 V. The magnetic field is 0.090 T. The radius of the path is 6.5×10^{-2} m. Find the mass of the calcium atom as a whole number of proton masses.

12. With an accelerating voltage of 73.5 V, a mass spectrometer produces ions with masses of 6.8×10^{-26} kg that move in a circular path with radius of 8.6×10^{-2} m in a 6.5×10^{-2} T magnetic field.

    a. What is the charge on one ion?

    b. How many electrons have been removed by the spectrometer to provide the ion?

13. A beam of singly ionized chlorine ions is sent through a mass spectrometer. The values are $B = 0.10$ T, $r = 4.9 \times 10^{-2}$ m, $q = 1.6 \times 10^{-19}$ C, and $V = 33$ V. Find the mass of the chlorine as a whole number of protons.

14. In Problem 13 you found the mass of a chlorine isotope. Another chlorine isotope has 37 proton masses. How far from the first isotope would these ions land on the photographic film in the spectrometer?

15. What length antenna would be best to transmit microwaves of wavelength of 2.4 cm?

16. The radio wave generated by Heinrich Hertz to demonstrate the transmission of radio waves had a frequency of 1.0×10^9 Hz. What length antenna would you use to detect this frequency?

27 Quantum Theory

1. When light falls on a photoelectronic surface, the stopping potential required to prevent current through the photocell is 3.5 V.

   a. What is the kinetic energy given to the electrons by the incident light. Give the answer in J and eV.

   b. What is the speed of the electrons?

2. The maximum kinetic energy given to electrons by incident light is 4.5 eV. What is the stopping voltage that prevents electrons from leaving the photocell?

3. A certain metal has a threshold frequency of 1.5×10^{14} Hz.

   a. What is the work function of the metal in J and eV?

   b. The metal is irradiated with light of wavelength 3.0×10^2 nm. What is the kinetic energy of the photoelectrons in eV?

4. Light shines on a metal surface in a photocell that has a work function of 1.4 eV. The energy of the most energetic electrons emitted is 0.89 eV. What is the wavelength of the light. In what part of the electromagnetic spectrum is that wavelength?

5. The stopping voltage in a photoelectric experiment is 5.3 V. Calculate the kinetic energy of the electrons as they are emitted.

6. The work function of a metal is 6.4 eV. Calculate the threshold frequency of the metal.

7. A metal has a threshold frequency of 3.3×10^{14} Hz. You shine a light with a frequency of 2.0×10^{15} Hz on the metal. Calculate the maximum energy of the ejected electrons.

8. Calculate the final velocity of an electron accelerated from rest across a potential difference of 60.0 V.

9. Calculate the de Broglie wavelength of a car of mass 1570 kg, traveling at a speed of 35 m/s. Why does the car not exhibit wave properties?

10. A ball with a mass of 0.55 kg is moving with a speed of 7600 m/s. Find the de Broglie wavelength.

11. Compare the de Broglie wavelengths of an electron and a proton, both moving at a speed of 6.0×10^4 m/s.

12. Find the de Broglie wavelength of an electron crossing a potential difference of 2.00×10^4 V in a television set.

13. The electrons in an electron microscope are accelerated through a potential difference of 5.0×10^4 V. Compare the wavelengths to the wavelengths of visible light.

14. Through what voltage must an electron be accelerated to obtain a de Broglie wavelength of 6.54×10^{-7} m?

15. Calculate the de Broglie wavelength of a 10.0-g bullet with a velocity of 7.0×10^2 m/s.

28 The Atom

1. What is the radius of the orbital associated with the energy level E_5 of the hydrogen atom?

2. a. Determine the energy associated with the 6th and 8th energy levels of the hydrogen atom.
   b. Determine the energy of the photon emitted as the electron drops from the 8th to the 6th level.
   c. Calculate the frequencies of the photons emitted.
   d. Calculate the wavelength of the photon emitted

3. a. How much energy must be absorbed to excite an electron from E_2 to E_6?
   b. What is the wavelength of the energy?

4. An atom drops from -9.32 eV to -7.60 eV.
   a. What is the energy of the photon emitted by the atom?
   b. What is the frequency of the photon?
   c. What is the wavelength of the photon?

5. The wavelength emitted by a hydrogen atom in a down transition from the E_4 energy level is 9.7×10^{-8} m. To which energy level did the electron drop?

6. An electron drops from a higher energy level to the E_2 level in hydrogen. The frequency of the light given off is 6.20×10^{14} Hz. What is the energy level from which the electron dropped?

7. Upon absorbing a photon of light of frequency 2.46×10^{15} Hz, an electron in the 1st energy level of a hydrogen atom jumps to the 2nd energy level.
   a. How much energy does the electron have in the second level?
   b. What is the wavelength of the light emitted by the electron as it returns to the ground state?

8. What is the maximum wavelength possible for an electron with an orbital radius of 6.20×10^{-11} m? Assume $n = 1$.

For questions 9 through 11 use the following table, which shows the energies associated with the first five energy levels of the hydrogen atom.

n	E (eV)
1	−13.6
2	−3.40
3	−1.51
4	−0.850
5	−0.544

9. How much energy in eV must by absorbed by an electron in the 1st energy level to jump to the 3rd energy level?

10. a. Determine the frequency of light emitted as an electron in the third energy level of the excited atom returns to the ground level.
    b. Determine the wavelength of the light.

11. Calculate the orbital radius associated with the 4th energy level.

Physics: Principles and Problems

29 Solid State Electronics

1. The forbidden gap in germanium is 0.7 eV. Electromagnetic waves striking the germanium cause electrons to jump from the valence band to the conduction band. What is the longest wavelength of radiation that could excite an electron in this way?

   Recall that $E = \dfrac{1240 \text{ eV} \cdot \text{nm}}{\lambda}$.

2. A light-emitting diode (LED) produces violet light with a wavelength of 430 nm when an electron moves from the conduction band to the valence band. Find the width of the forbidden gap in eV in this diode.

3. How many free electrons exist in a cubic centimeter of calcium? Its density is 1.55 g/cm^3, its atomic mass is 40.08 g/mole, and there are two free electrons per atom.

4. Name two elements that could be used as the second dopant used to make a diode, if the first dopant were phosphorus.

5. The voltage drop across a diode is 2.1 V when it is connected in series to a 275-Ω resistor and a battery, and there is a 36-mA current. What is the battery voltage?

6. A diode is connected to a 9.0-V battery through a 1160-Ω resistor. The current in the diode is 7.0 mA. What is the voltage drop across the diode?

7. The voltage drop across a diode is 1.5 V when it is connected in series to a 785-Ω resistor and a 6.0-V battery. What is the current in the diode?

Physics: Principles and Problems

30 The Nucleus

1. Three isotopes of nickel have mass numbers of 56, 59, and 67. The atomic number of nickel is 28. How many neutrons are in the nucleus of each of these isotopes?

2. An isotope of carbon has a mass number of 16. How many neutrons are in the nucleus of this isotope?

3. How many neutrons are in the cesium isotope $^{139}_{55}$Cs?

4. The atomic number of gold, Au, is 79. Write the symbols for three isotopes of gold that have 106, 111, and 114 neutrons.

5. How many neutrons are in the nucleus of an isotope of lead, Pb, that has a mass number of 214?

6. Write the nuclear equation for the transmutation of a radioactive isotope of Polonium, $^{211}_{84}$Po, into the lead isotope $^{207}_{82}$Pb with the emission of an alpha particle.

7. Write the nuclear equation for the alpha decay of a beryllium isotope, $^{8}_{4}$Be, into a helium isotope $^{4}_{2}$He.

8. Write the nuclear equation for the transmutation of a radioactive isotope of actinium, $^{225}_{89}$Ac, into a francium, Fr, isotope by the emission of an alpha particle.

9. Write the nuclear equation for the transmutation of a radioactive isotope of chlorine, $^{39}_{17}$Cl, into argon, $^{39}_{18}$Ar, by the emission of a beta particle and an antineutrino.

10. A radioactive iron isotope, $^{60}_{26}$Fe, can change into cobalt isotope $^{60}_{27}$Co by the emission of a beta particle and an antineutrino. Write the nuclear equation.

11. Write the nuclear equation for the beta decay of a radioactive isotope of potassium, $^{42}_{19}$K, into an isotope of calcium, Ca.

Refer to Figure 30-5 on page 699 of your text to solve the following problems.

12. Argon, $^{42}_{16}$Ar, has a half-life of 33 years. If a 4.0-g sample of the argon is produced, what will be the mass of the argon remaining after 99 years?

13. A sample of tin, $^{117}_{50}$Sn, has an activity of about 1×10^5 Bq. It has a half-life of 14 days. If a sample was purchased on the first of February, what would be its activity at the end of the month?

14. An isotope of manganese, $^{53}_{25}$Mn, has a half-life of 2×10^6 years. How would the activity in a rock sample now compare with the activity 5×10^5 years ago?

15. The mass of a neutron is 1.674×10^{-27} kg.
    a. Find the energy equivalent to the neutron's mass in joules.
    b. Convert this value to eV.

Physics: Principles and Problems Supplemental Problems • Chapter 30 57

31 Nuclear Applications

Use these values for the following problems.

mass of proton = 1.007825 u
mass of neutron = 1.008665 u
1 u = 931.49 MeV

1. A lithium isotope, $^{7}_{3}\text{Li}$, has a nuclear mass of 7.016005 u.
   a. Calculate the mass defect.
   b. Calculate the binding energy.

2. A carbon isotope, $^{14}_{6}\text{C}$, has a nuclear mass of 14.00324 u.
   a. Calculate the mass defect.
   b. Calculate the binding energy.

3. The isotope of chlorine that has 17 protons and 20 neutrons has a mass of 36.96590 u.
   a. Calculate its mass defect.
   b. Find the binding energy.

4. An isotope of cobalt, $^{60}_{27}\text{Co}$, has a mass of 59.93382 u.
   a. Find the mass defect.
   b. Find the binding energy.

5. The mass of an isotope of iron, $^{56}_{26}\text{Fe}$, is 55.93490 u.
   a. Find the mass defect.
   b. Find the binding energy.

6. The nucleus of a calcium isotope, $^{42}_{20}\text{Ca}$, is 41.95863 u.
   a. Calculate the mass defect.
   b. Calculate the binding energy.

Use Appendix F Table F-6 in the text to complete the following equations.

7. Write the nuclear equation when a radioisotope of francium, $^{221}_{87}\text{Fr}$, undergoes alpha decay to form an isotope of astatine, At.

8. Complete the following equation:
   $^{217}_{85}\text{At} \rightarrow ? + {}^{4}_{2}\text{He}$

9. Write the nuclear equation when a radioisotope of thorium, $^{229}_{90}\text{Th}$, undergoes alpha decay.

10. Write the nuclear equation when a radioactive isotope of platinum, $^{197}_{78}\text{Pt}$, undergoes beta decay to form a stable isotope of gold, Au.

11. Write the nuclear equation for the beta decay of a radioactive isotope of cobalt, $^{62}_{27}\text{Co}$.

12. Complete the following nuclear equation:
    $^{55}_{24}\text{Cr} \rightarrow ? + {}^{0}_{-1}\text{e} + {}^{0}_{0}\bar{\nu}$.

13. Write the nuclear equation for the beta decay of a radioisotope of phosphorus, $^{34}_{15}\text{P}$.

14. Write the equation for the beta decay of a radioactive isotope of bromine, $^{80}_{35}\text{Br}$.

Physics: Principles and Problems

Supplemental Problems

ANSWER KEY

ANSWER KEY

Chapter 2

1. Express the following quantities in scientific notation.

   a. 22 300 kg

   2.23×10^4 kg

   b. 401 kg

   4.01×10^2 kg

   c. 0.57 kg

   5.7×10^{-1} kg

   d. 0.000 084 kg

   8.4×10^{-5} kg

   e. 0.000 000 044 9 kg

   4.49×10^{-8} kg

2. Convert each of the following measurements as directed.

   a. 11 m to cm

   $(11 \text{ m}) \times \left(\dfrac{100 \text{ cm}}{1 \text{ m}}\right)$

   $= \dfrac{11 \text{ m} \times 100 \text{ cm}}{1 \text{ m}}$

   $= 1100$ cm

   b. 230 ms to s

   $(230 \text{ ms}) \times \left(\dfrac{1 \text{ s}}{1000 \text{ ms}}\right)$

   $= \dfrac{230 \text{ ms} \times 1 \text{ s}}{1000 \text{ ms}}$

   $= 0.23$ s

   c. 0.133 kg to g

   $(0.133 \text{ kg}) \times \left(\dfrac{1000 \text{ g}}{1 \text{ kg}}\right)$

   $= \dfrac{0.133 \text{ kg} \times 1000 \text{ g}}{1 \text{ kg}}$

   $= 133$ kg

   d. 8.5 dm to cm

   $(8.5 \text{ dm}) \times \left(\dfrac{1 \text{ m}}{10 \text{ dm}}\right) \times \left(\dfrac{100 \text{ cm}}{1 \text{ m}}\right)$

   $= \dfrac{8.5 \text{ dm} \times 1 \text{ m} \times 100 \text{ cm}}{10 \text{ dm} \times 1 \text{ m}}$

   $= 85$ cm

3. Solve the following problems and express the answers in scientific notation.

   a. 32.1 cm + 2.1 cm

   32.1 cm + 2.1 cm = 34.2 cm

   $= 34.2 \times 10^0$ cm

   $= 3.42 \times 10^1$ cm

   b. 4×10^3 kg + 3×10^3 kg

   $= 7 \times 10^3$ kg

   c. 8.9×10^2 mm + 3.4×10^2 mm

   $= 12.3 \times 10^2$ mm

   $= 1.23 \times 10^3$ mm

   d. 63.0×10^2 ms − 21×10^1 ms

   63.0×10^2 ms − 2.1×10^2 ms

   $= 60.9 \times 10^2$ ms

   $= 6.09 \times 10^3$ ms

   e. 59×10^1 m − 0.20 km

   $= 59 \times 10^1 \text{ m} - 0.20 \text{ km}\left(\dfrac{1000 \text{ m}}{1 \text{ km}}\right)$

   $= 5.9 \times 10^2$ m − 2.0×10^2 m

   $= 3.9 \times 10^2$ m

4. Find the value of each of the following quantities and express it in scientific notation.

   a. $(2.00 \times 10^1 \text{ mm})(2.10 \times 10^1 \text{ mm})(2.20 \times 10^1 \text{ mm})$

   $= 9.24 \times 10^{(1+1+1)}$ mm³

   $= 9.24 \times 10^3$ mm³

   b. $(6.96 \times 10^2 \text{ kg})(1.2 \times 10^{-1} \text{ m/s})$

   $5.8 \times 10^{(2+-1)}$ kg·m/s

   $= 5.8 \times 10^1$ kg·m/s

   c. $\dfrac{35.84 \times 10^3 \text{ m}}{56 \text{ s}}$

   $= \dfrac{3.584 \times 10^3 \text{ m}}{5.6 \times 10^1 \text{ s}}$

   $= 0.64 \times 10^{(3-1)}$ m/s $= 0.64 \times 10^2$ m/s

   $= 6.4 \times 10^1$ m/s

62 Supplemental Problems Answer Key · Physics: Principles and Problems

ANSWER KEY

d. $$\frac{(2.5 \times 10^{-2} \text{ kg}) \times (1.7 \times 10^{-2} \text{ m})}{(8.5 \times 10^{-5} \text{ s})}$$

$$= \frac{(4.25 \times 10^{-4} \text{ kh·m})}{(8.5 \times 10^{-5} \text{ s})}$$

$= 0.50 \times 10^{(-4 - -5)}$ kg·m/s

$= 0.50 \times 10^1$ kg·m/s

$= 5.0$ kg·m/s

e. $$\frac{(4.2 \times 10^1 \text{ kg})}{(3.5 \times 10^4 \text{ cm})(2.0 \times 10^2 \text{ dm})(1.5 \times 10^{-1} \text{ m})}$$

$$= \frac{(4.2 \times 10^1 \text{ kg})}{(3.5 \times 10^4 \text{ cm})(\frac{1 \text{ m}}{100 \text{ cm}})(2.0 \times 10^2 \text{ dm})(\frac{1 \text{ m}}{10 \text{ dm}})(1.5 \times 10^{-1} \text{ m})}$$

$$= \frac{(4.2 \times 10^1 \text{ kg})}{(3.5 \times 10^4 \text{ cm})(10^{-2} \text{ m/cm})(2.0 \times 10^2 \text{ dm})(10^{-1} \text{ m/dm})(1.5 \times 10^{-1} \text{ m})}$$

$$= \frac{(4.2 \times 10^1 \text{ kg})}{(10.5 \times 10^{(4 + -2 + 2 + -1 + -1)} \text{ m}^3)}$$

$$= \frac{(4.2 \times 10^1 \text{ kg})}{10.5 \times 10^2 \text{ m}^3}$$

$= 0.40 \times 10^{(1 - 2)}$ kg/m³

$= 0.40 \times 10^{-1}$ kg/m³

$= 4.0 \times 10^{-2}$ kg/m³

5. State the number of significant digits in each measurement and express the value in scientific notation.

   a. 110 m

      2; 1.1×10^2 m

   b. 0.2°C

      1; 2×10^{-1}°C

   c. 0.090 11 kg

      4; 9.011×10^{-2} kg

   d. 52.5×10^{-3} mm

      3; 5.25×10^{-2} mm

   e. 600.0 N

      4; 6.000×10^2 N

   f. 20.40 m/s

      4; 2.040×10^1 m/s

   g. 0.71 ns

      2; 7.1×10^{-1} ns

h. 0.06 kg

1; 6×10^{-2} kg

i. 7040 m

3; 7.04×10^3 m

6. Add or subtract as indicated and express the answer in scientific notation with the correct number of significant digits.

   a. 9902 m + 201 m

   9902 m + 201 m = 10 103 m

   1.0103×10^4 m

   b. 5.060 cm + 32.07 cm

   5.060 cm + 32.07 cm = 37.130 cm

   = 37.13 cm

   = 3.713×10^1 cm

   c. 1.5 km − 355 m

   1.5 km − 355 m

   1500 m − 355 m = 1145 m

   = 1100 m

   = 1.1×10^3 m, or 1.1 km

   d. 5.5×10^{-1} mm + 2×10^{-3} cm

   5.5×10^{-1} mm + 2×10^{-3} cm

   0.55 mm + 0.02 mm = 0.57 mm

   = 5.7×10^{-1} mm

7. Evaluate the following quantities and state each answer in scientific notation with the correct number of significant digits.

   a. $(4.2 \times 10^1 \text{ m})^2$

   $(4.2 \times 10^1 \text{ m})^2 = 17.64 \times 10^2$ m²

   1.8×10^3 m²

   b. 1200 m/10.0 s

   1200 m/10.0 s = 120.0 m/s

   = 1.2×10^2 m/s

   c. (17 mm)(17.6 cm)

   (17 mm)(17.6 cm) = (17 mm)(176 mm)

   = $(1.7 \times 10^1$ mm$)(1.76 \times 10^2$ mm$)$

   = 2.992×10^3 mm

   = 3.0×10^3 mm

   d. 0.1387 kg/[(0.121 m)(0.021 m)(2.00 m)]

   0.1387 kg/[(0.121 m)(0.021 m)(2.00 m)]

   = 27.292402 kg/m³

   = 2.8×10^1 kg/m³

8. Table 2-1 shows the volume of blood delivered at various intervals during a routine blood transfusion.

TABLE 2-1	
Time ($\times 10^2$ s)	Volume (cm³)
0.00	0.0
1.00	6.0
2.00	12.1
3.00	17.9
4.00	23.9
5.00	29.9
6.00	35.9

   a. Plot the values given in the table and draw the curve that best fits all points.

   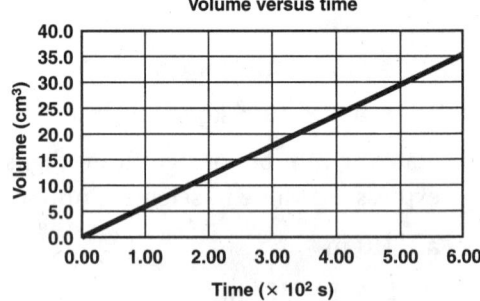

   b. Describe the resulting curve.

   The curve is a straight line.

   c. Use the graph to write an equation relating volume to time.

   $V = rt$, where r, the slope, has a value of 5.98×10^{-2} cm³/s

ANSWER KEY

e. In how many minutes will 5.00×10^2 cm³ of blood transfuse at this rate?

$V = rt$

$t = \dfrac{V}{r} = \dfrac{5.00 \times 10^2 \text{ cm}^3}{5.98 \times 10^{-2} \text{ cm}^3/\text{s}}$

$= 8.36 \times 10^3$ s

$= (8.36 \times 10^3 \text{ s}) \times (1 \text{ min}/60 \text{ s})$

$= 139$ min

9. In an experiment, a student dropped tiny aluminum spheres of varying radii into a tall cylinder of glycerin and then measured the speed at which they fell. Table 2-2 shows the data.

TABLE 2-2	
Sphere radius ($\times 10^{-2}$ m)	Maximum speed ($\times 10^2$ m/s)
0.20	0.15
0.40	0.61
0.60	1.35
0.80	2.42
1.00	3.79

a. Plot the values given in the table and draw the curve that best fits all points.

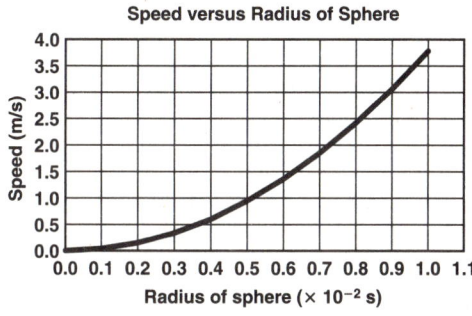

b. The equation of the line is $s = ar^2$, where a is a constant for glycerin and aluminum. Describe the curve.

The curve is a parabola.

c. What is the numerical value of a?

$a = \dfrac{s}{r^2} = \dfrac{(3.79 \times 10^2)}{(1.00 \times 10^{-2})^2}$

$= 3.79 \times 10^{(2 - -4)}$

$= 3.79 \times 10^6$

d. What are the units of a?

$a = \dfrac{s}{r^2} = \dfrac{\text{m/s}}{(\text{m})^2} = \dfrac{\text{m/s}}{\text{m}^2}$

$= \dfrac{1}{\text{m} \cdot \text{s}} = (\text{m} \cdot \text{s})^{-1}$

10. If small-diameter glass tubes, called capillary tubes, are placed in water, the water rises in the tubes. Table 2-3 shows the radii of the capillary tubes and the average height that the water rose in each tube.

TABLE 2-3	
Radius ($\times 10^{-5}$ m)	Height of water column ($\times 10^{-2}$ m)
2.0	72.5
4.0	36.2
6.0	24.2
8.0	18.1
10.0	14.3

a. Plot the values given in the table and draw the curve that best fits all points.

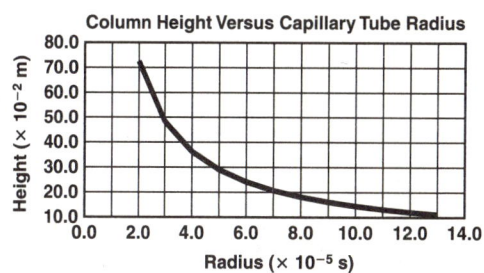

b. Describe the resulting curve.

The curve is a hyperbola.

c. According to the graph, what is the relationship between the height to which the water rises and the radius of the capillary tube?

The height of the water column varies inversely with the radius of the capillary tube.

Physics: Principles and Problems

d. Write the equation relating the height of the water column and the radius of the capillary tube. Give the value of the constant to three significant digits.

$h = \dfrac{c}{r}$; c = constant = 1.45×10^{-5}

e. What are the units of c?

m^2

Chapter 3

1. A truck is traveling at a constant speed as shown below.

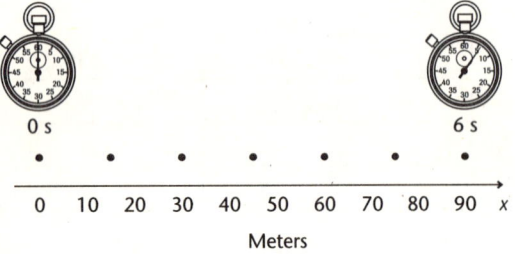

Sketch the motion diagram on a separate piece of paper and draw the displacements of the truck at 2 seconds and 5 seconds. Label the displacements d_0 and d_1, respectively. Draw and label the displacement, Δd, that the truck underwent from 2 to 5 seconds.

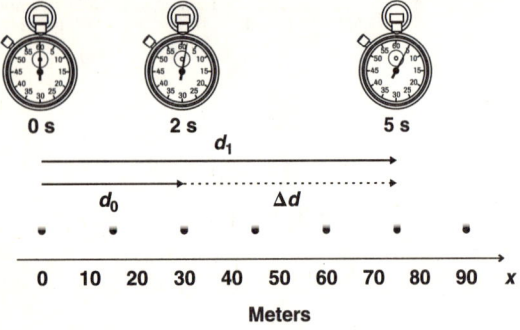

2. The motion diagrams below represent an SUV and a car each traveling in the same direction.

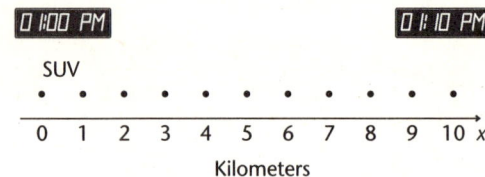

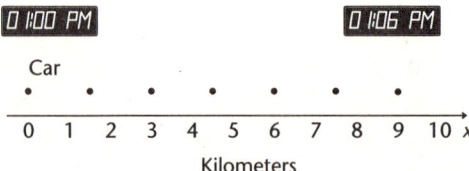

Sketch the motion diagrams on a separate piece of paper and answer the following questions.

a. Which vehicle has the greater speed? How do you know?

   The car has a greater speed. The distance between consecutive dots is greater than that of the SUV for equal time intervals.

b. Draw the displacement of each vehicle after 4 seconds and the vector representing the displacement of the car with respect to the SUV.

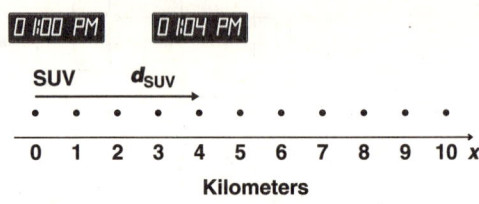

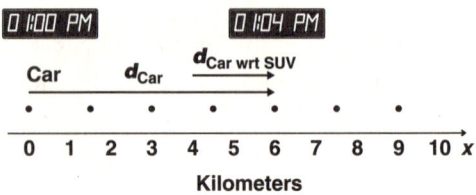

c. The SUV and car are traveling in opposite directions with the same speeds as before. Draw and label the displacement of each vehicle 3 seconds after they pass each other. Assume the SUV is traveling in the positive *x*-direction to the right. Then draw the vector representing the displacement of the car with respect to the SUV at 3 seconds.

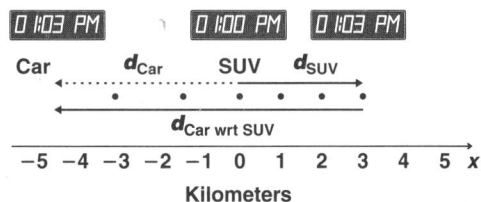

d. Redraw your answers to Problem 2c assuming the car is traveling in the positive *x*-direction to the left.

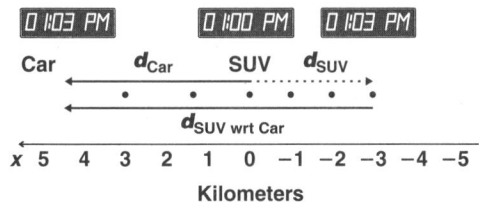

e. Compare the magnitude of the vector representing the displacement of the car with respect to the SUV with the magnitude of the vector representing the displacement of the SUV with respect to the car at 3 seconds.

The magnitudes are equal.

For Questions 3–6, create pictorial and physical models. Do not solve the problems.

3. A helicopter ascends at a constant speed of 5 m/s. How far does it rise in 5 seconds?

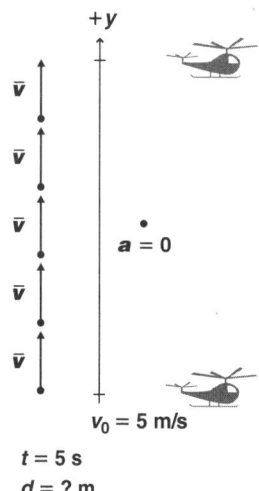

4. An empty toy wagon reaches the bottom of a hill and rolls onto the level ground at a speed of 1.5 m/s. How long will it take the wagon to come to a stop if its acceleration is -0.6 m/s^2?

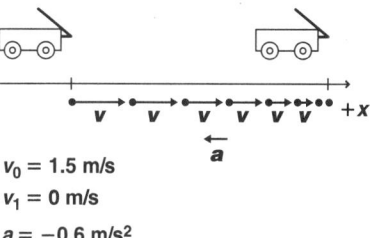

ANSWER KEY

5. A diver jumps vertically with a velocity of 4.0 m/s from a platform and enters the water 1.9 seconds later. How high is the platform? (**Hint:** The acceleration is the same whether the diver is moving up or down.)

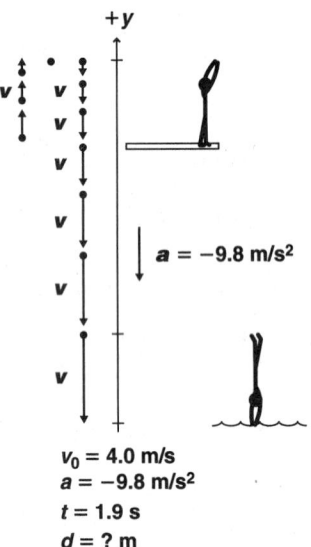

$v_0 = 4.0$ m/s
$a = -9.8$ m/s^2
$t = 1.9$ s
$d = ?$ m

6. A driver backs a car at a velocity of -2.3 m/s from a driveway onto a street. If the acceleration of the car is 0.8 m/s^2, how far onto the street does the car move before it comes to a stop?

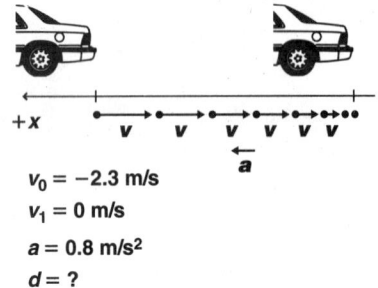

$v_0 = -2.3$ m/s
$v_1 = 0$ m/s
$a = 0.8$ m/s^2
$d = ?$

Chapter 4

1. A soccer player runs forward a distance of 4 m, reverses direction and runs a distance of 3 m, and then reverses direction again and runs a distance of 8 m.

   a. What distance does the player run?

   15 m

   b. What is his displacement?

   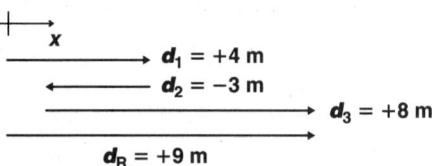

   9 m forward

2. A jogger starts a three-part jog by running 0.24 km north, then 0.16 km east, and finally back to her starting point along a straight-line path. Graphically determine the jogger's third displacement.

   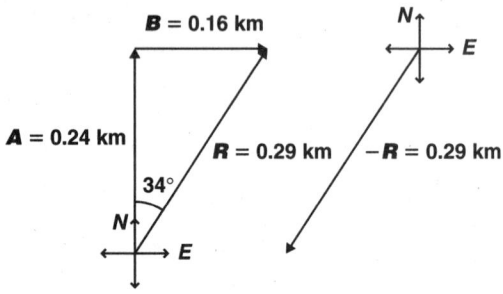

   $-R = 0.29$ km 56° south of west

3. After takeoff, an air-traffic controller locates a small plane 12.0 km southeast of the airport. At this point, the plane turns 20.0° to the east of its original flight path and flies 21.0 km. What is the magnitude of the plane's displacement from the airport?

   $R^2 = A^2 + B^2 - 2AB \cos \theta$
   $ = (12.0 \text{ km})^2 + (21.0 \text{ km})^2$
   $ - 2(12.0 \text{ km})(21.0 \text{ km})\cos 160.0°$
   $ = 144 \text{ km}^2 + 441 \text{ km}^2$
   $ - 504 \text{ km}^2(\cos 160.0°)$
   $R^2 = 1059 \text{ km}^2$
   $R = \sqrt{1059 \text{ km}^2}$
   $R = 32.5$ km

4. A gymnast tumbles forward 4.0 m, does cartwheels to the left for 6.0 m, and climbs a vertical rope to a height of 3.0 m. What is the magnitude of the gymnast's displacement?

   $R_{xy} = \sqrt{(A^2 + B^2)} = \sqrt{(4.0 \text{ m})^2 + (6.0 \text{ m})^2}$
   $R_{xy} = 7.2$ m
   $R_{xyz} = \sqrt{(R_{xy}^2 + C^2)}$

68 Supplemental Problems Answer Key   Physics: Principles and Problems

$= \sqrt{(7.2 \text{ m})^2 + (3.0 \text{ m})^2}$

$R_{xyz} = 7.8$ m

Second method:

Knowing that $R_{xy} = \sqrt{(A^2 + B^2)}$

$R_{xyz} = \sqrt{(R_{xy}^2 + C^2)}$

$= \sqrt{(\sqrt{(A^2 + B^2)})^2 + (C)^2}$

$R_{xyz} = \sqrt{(A^2 + B^2 + C^2)}$

$= \sqrt{(4.0 \text{ m})^2 + (6.0 \text{ m})^2 + (3.0 \text{ m})^2}$

$R_{xyz} = 7.8$ m

5. Graphically determine the difference in displacement, Δd, for each pair of displacements below.

   a. $d_1 = +2.0$ m, $d_2 = +3.0$ m

   $\Delta d = +1.0$ m

   b. $d_1 = +2.0$ m, $d_2 = +2.0$ m

   $\Delta d = 0.0$ m

   c. $d_1 = +2.0$ m, $d_2 = -2.0$ m

   $\Delta d = -4.0$ m

   d. $d_1 = 2.0$ m at 35° north of east
      $d_2 = 3.0$ m at 25° south of east

   $\Delta d = 2.6$ m at 66° south of east

6. Two cars approach a crossroad 36 m ahead. Car A is traveling east at 9 m/s and car B is traveling south at 12 m/s.

   a. What is the location of car B relative to car A?

   $R = \sqrt{(36 \text{ m})^2 + (36 \text{ m})^2}$

   $R = 51$ m

   $\tan \theta = \dfrac{B}{A} = \dfrac{36 \text{ m}}{36 \text{ m}} = 1.0$

   $\theta = \tan^{-1}(1.0) = 45°$

   $R_{\text{car B relative to car A}} = 51$ m at 45° north of east

   b. What is the location of car B relative to car A 2.0 seconds later?

   Car A moves 18 m in 2 seconds and Car B moves 24 m.

   $R = \sqrt{(36 \text{ m} - 18 \text{ m})^2 + (36 \text{ m} - 24 \text{ m})^2}$

   $= \sqrt{(18 \text{ m})^2 + (12 \text{ m})^2}$

   $R = 22$ m

   $\tan \theta = \dfrac{B}{A} = \dfrac{12 \text{ m}}{18 \text{ m}} = 0.67$

   $\theta = \tan^{-1}(0.67) = 34°$

   $R_{\text{car B relative to car A}} = 22$ m at 34° north of east

c. Where does the car that first reaches the crossroad locate the other car the moment the former passes through the crossroad?

Car B, the first car to pass through the crossroad, passes through at 3.0 s. Car A travels 27 m in 3.0 s and is 9 m from the crossroad.

$R_{\text{car A relative to car B}}$ = 9 m west

7. The moving sidewalk at an airport has a speed of 0.9 m/s toward the departure gate.

a. A man is walking toward the departure gate on the moving sidewalk at a speed of 1.0 m/s relative to the sidewalk. What is the velocity of the man relative to a woman standing off the moving sidewalk?

$v_{\text{man relative to woman}}$
= $v_{\text{man relative to moving sidewalk}}$
+ $v_{\text{moving sidewalk relative to ground}}$
+ $v_{\text{ground relative to woman}}$

But $v_{\text{ground relative to woman}}$
= $-v_{\text{woman relative to ground}}$

So,

$v_{\text{man relative to woman}}$
= $v_{\text{man relative to moving sidewalk}}$
+ $v_{\text{moving sidewalk relative to ground}}$
− $v_{\text{ground relative to woman}}$
= 1.0 m/s + 0.9 m/s − (0 m/s)

$v_{\text{man relative to woman}}$ = 1.9 m/s toward the departure gate

b. On a similar moving sidewalk moving in the opposite direction, a child walks toward the terminal at a speed of 0.4 m/s relative to the sidewalk. What is the velocity of the man relative to the child?

$v_{\text{man relative to child}}$
= $v_{\text{man relative to moving sidewalk 1}}$
+ $v_{\text{moving sidewalk 1 relative to ground}}$
+ $v_{\text{ground relative to moving sidewalk 2}}$
+ $v_{\text{moving sidewalk 2 relative to child}}$

But, $v_{\text{ground relative to moving sidewalk 2}}$
= $-v_{\text{moving sidewalk 2 relative to ground}}$

and $v_{\text{moving sidewalk 2 relative to child}}$
= $-v_{\text{child relative to moving sidewalk 2}}$

So, $v_{\text{man relative to child}}$
= $v_{\text{man relative to moving sidewalk 1}}$
+ $v_{\text{moving sidewalk 1 relative to ground}}$
− $v_{\text{moving sidewalk 2 relative to ground}}$
− $v_{\text{child relative to moving sidewalk 2}}$

So, $v_{\text{man relative to child}}$
= 1.0 m/s + 0.9 m/s − (−0.9 m/s)
− (−0.4 m/s)

$v_{\text{man relative to child}}$ = 3.2 m/s toward the departure gate.

8. A kite is tethered to a stake on a beach. The wind has a constant velocity of 16 km/h at an angle of 15° from the horizontal relative to the beach. Find the components of the kite's velocity relative to the wind.

$v_{\text{x wind}} = v_{\text{wind}} \cos \theta$ = (16 km/h) cos(15°)
$v_{\text{x wind}}$ = 15 km/h in the direction of the wind

$v_{\text{y wind}} = v_{\text{wind}} \sin \theta$ = (16 km/h) sin(15°)
$v_{\text{y wind}}$ = 4.1 km/h upward

$v_{\text{kite relative to wind}}$
= $v_{\text{kite relative to beach}}$
+ $v_{\text{beach relative to wind}}$

$v_{\text{beach relative to wind}} = -v_{\text{wind}}$

$v_{\text{kite relative to wind}}$
= $v_{\text{kite relative to beach}} + -v_{\text{wind}}$

$v_{\text{x kite relative to wind}}$
= $v_{\text{x kite relative to beach}} + -v_{\text{x wind}}$
= 0 km/h + −15 km/h

$v_{\text{x kite relative to wind}}$ = −15 km/h

$v_{\text{y kite relative to wind}}$
= $v_{\text{y kite relative to beach}} + -v_{\text{y wind}}$
= 0 km/h + −4.1 km/h

$v_{\text{y kite relative to wind}}$ = −4.1 km/h

9. A hiker starts by walking along a straight path. He then turns and walks 260.0 m west. If he finds he is located 360.0 m exactly north of his starting point, what was his displacement along the path?

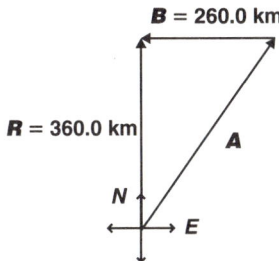

$R_x = 0.0$ m, $R_y = 360.0$ m
$B_x = -260.0$ m, $B_y = 0.0$ m
$R = A + B, A = R - B$
$A_x = R_x - B_x = 0.0$ m $- -260.0$ m
$A_x = 260.0$ m
$A_y = R_y - B_y = 360.0$ m $- 0.0$ m
$A_y = 360.0$ m
$A = \sqrt{(260.0 \text{ m})^2 + (360.0 \text{ m})^2}$
$A = 444.1$ m
$\tan\theta = \dfrac{B}{R} = \dfrac{360.0 \text{ m}}{260.0 \text{ m}} = 1.3846$
$\theta = \tan^{-1}(1.3846) = 54.2°$
A = 444.1 m 54.2° east of north

10. A hammer slides down a roof that makes a 40.0° angle with the horizontal. What are the magnitudes of the components of the hammer's velocity at the edge of the roof if it is moving at a speed of 4.25 m/s?

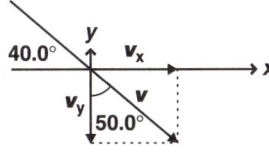

$v_x = v \sin\theta = (4.25 \text{ m/s})\sin(50.0°)$
$v_x = 3.26$ m/s
$v_y = v \cos\theta = (4.25 \text{ m/s})\cos(50.0°)$
$v_y = -2.73$ m/s

Chapter 5

1. A biker starts a trip and rides at a constant velocity of +12 km/h for 0.20 h. For the next 0.10 h he bikes at an increased constant velocity and finds that he is at a rest stop +4.8 km from his starting point. In the next 0.20 h, half of which he rests, his average velocity is +9.0 km/h.

   a. Construct a d-t graph for the trip.

   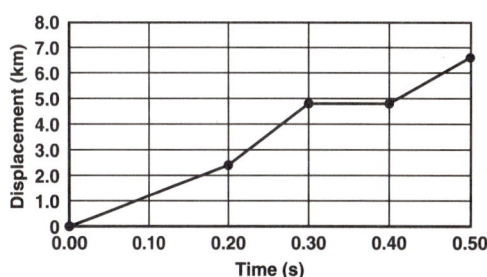

   0.00 to 0.20 h
   $d_0 = 0.0$ km
   $\Delta d = d_0 + vt$
   $\quad\quad = 0.0$ km $+ (12$ km/h$)(0.20$ h$)$
   $\Delta d = +2.4$ km $= d_2 - d_0$
   $d_2 = 2.4$ km $+ 0.0$ km
   $d_2 = +2.4$ km

   0.20 h to 0.30 h
   $d_3 = 4.8$ km

   0.30 h to 0.50 h
   $\Delta d = d_3 + vt$
   $\quad\quad = 4.8$ km $+ (9.0$ km/h$)(0.20$ h$)$
   $\Delta d = 6.6$ km $= d_5 - d_0$
   $d_5 = 6.6$ km $+ 0.0$ km
   $d_5 = +6.6$ km

   0.30 h to 0.40 h
   $\Delta d = 0$ km $= d_4 - d_3$
   $d_4 = d_3 = 4.8$ km

b. What is his average velocity for the trip?

$$\bar{v} = \frac{\Delta d}{\Delta t} = \frac{+6.6 \text{ km} - 0.0 \text{ km}}{0.50 \text{ h} - 0.00 \text{ h}}$$

$$\bar{v} = +13 \text{ km/h}$$

2. Alice and Faye are located +18 m from a flagpole. They begin running with constant velocities of −2.0 m/s and −3.0 m/s, respectively. At 10.0 s, Faye changes her velocity and meets Alice 3.0 seconds later.

  a. Plot the motion of each girl on the same d-t graph.

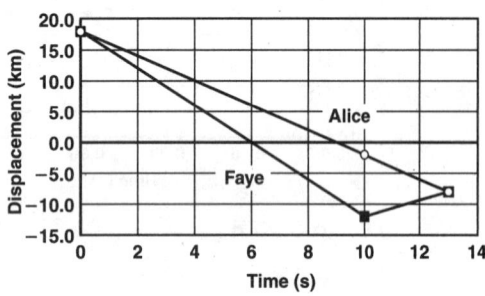

  b. Where do they meet?

  −8.0 m (8.0 m on the opposite side of the flagpole)

  c. What is Faye's average velocity for the last 3.0 seconds?

$$\bar{v} = \frac{\Delta d}{t} = \frac{d_1 - d_0}{t}$$

$$= \frac{-8.0 \text{ m} - (-12.0 \text{ m})}{3.0 \text{ s}}$$

$$\bar{v} = \frac{4.0 \text{ m}}{3.0 \text{ s}}$$

$$\bar{v} = 1.3 \text{ m/s}$$

3. Seth starts a half-hour canoe trip by paddling at a velocity of +5.0 km/h relative to the river for 0.20 h. He rests for 0.05 h and then paddles at a velocity of −3.0 km/h relative to the river for the remainder of the half hour.

  a. Construct a d-t graph of his motion.

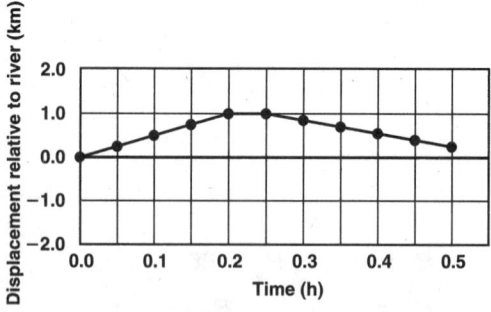

  b. Construct a d-t graph of Seth's motion relative to the shore if he paddles upstream in a river that has a velocity of +2.0 km/h. On the same graph plot Seth's motion if he paddles downstream in the same river.

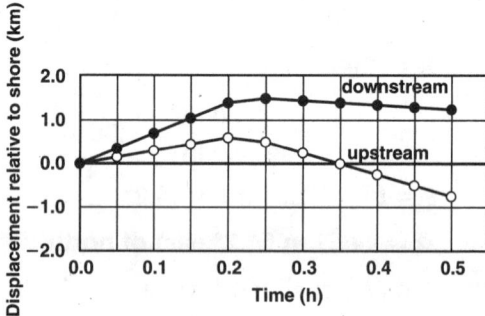

4. One day a rabbit challenged a skunk to a race. The following v-t graph shows the motion of a crazy rabbit during the race.

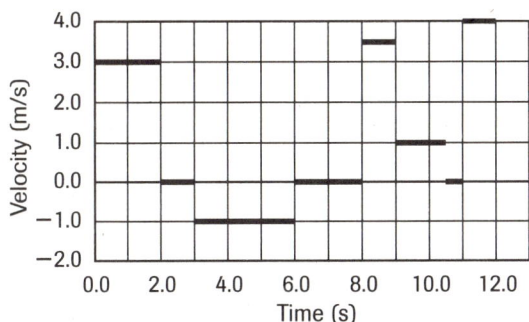

If the rabbit crosses the finish line at 12.0 s, what average velocity did the skunk maintain to cross the finish line a moment before the rabbit?

The displacement of the rabbit is the sum of the area ($d = vt$) under the curve of each segment of the v-t graph.

d = (3.0 m/s)(2.0 s) + (0 m/s)(1.0 s)
   + (−1 m/s)(3.0 s) + (0 m/s)(2.0 s)
   + (3.5 m/s)(1.0 s) + (1.0 m/s)(1.5 s)
   + (0 m/s)(0.5 s) + (4.0 m/s)(1.0 s)

d = 12.0 m. Thus, the course is 12 m long.

$$\bar{v}_{rabbit} = \frac{\Delta d}{t} = \frac{d_1 - d_0}{t} = \frac{12\text{ m} - 0\text{ m}}{12.0\text{ s}}$$

$\bar{v}_{rabbit}$ = 1.0 m/s

For the skunk to win the race, its average velocity must be slightly greater than 1.0 m/s.

5. Look at the v-t graph of a remote-controlled toy car below. At $t = 0.0$ s, the car is located at = +10.0 cm.

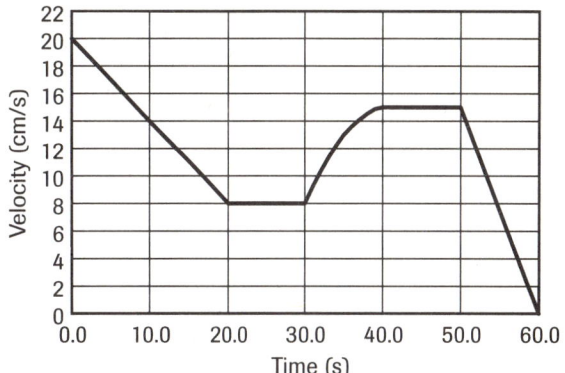

a. In which time interval or intervals does the car have a constant velocity?

20.0 to 30.0 s, 40.0 to 50.0 s

b. In which time interval or intervals does the car have constant positive acceleration?

The car never has a constant positive acceleration.

c. In which time interval or intervals does the car have constant negative acceleration?

0.0 to 20.0 s, 50.0 to 60.0 s

d. In which time interval or intervals is the car moving forward?

In all time intervals the car is moving forward.

e. What is the magnitude of the acceleration at $t = 35.0$ s?

Answers will vary due to orientation of the tangent line.

$$a = \frac{\text{rise}}{\text{run}} = \frac{16.2\text{ cm/s} - 10.0\text{ cm/s}}{40.0\text{ s} - 30.0\text{ s}}$$

a = 0.620 cm/s^2

6. A golf ball leaves a tee at a speed of 2.0×10^2 km/h after being accelerated for 0.56 ms.

   a. What is the ball's average acceleration in m/s²?

   $$\left(\frac{2.0 \times 10^2 \text{ km}}{\text{h}}\right)\left(\frac{1000 \text{ m}}{1 \text{ km}}\right)\left(\frac{1 \text{ h}}{3600 \text{ s}}\right)$$
   $$= 56 \text{ m/s}$$

   $$a = \frac{\Delta v}{t} = \frac{v_1 - v_0}{t}$$
   $$= \frac{56 \text{ m/s} - 0 \text{ m/s}}{5.6 \times 10^{-4} \text{ s}}$$
   $$a = 1.0 \times 10^5 \text{ m/s}^2$$

   b. How far does it move in this time interval?

   $$d = d_0 + v_0 t + \frac{1}{2}at^2$$
   $$= 0.0 \text{ m} + (0.0 \text{ m/s})(5.6 \times 10^{-4} \text{ s})$$
   $$+ \frac{1}{2}(1.0 \times 10^5 \text{ m/s}^2)(5.6 \times 10^{-4} \text{ s})^2$$
   $$d = 1.6 \times 10^{-2} \text{ m}$$

7. A flea develops an acceleration of 2.0×10^3 m/s² during takeoff. After takeoff the flea reaches a height of 36 mm.

   a. How fast does the flea leave the ground?

   $$v^2 = v_0^2 + 2g(d - d_0)$$
   $$v = \sqrt{v_0^2 + 2g(d - d_0)}$$
   $$v = \sqrt{(0.00 \text{ m/s}) + 2(-9.80 \text{ m/s}^2)}$$
   $$\overline{(0.0 \text{ m} - 3.6 \times 10^{-2} \text{ m})}$$
   $$v = 0.84 \text{ m/s}$$

   b. How long does the take-off acceleration last?

   $$a = \frac{\Delta v}{t} = \frac{v_1 - v_0}{t}$$
   $$t = \frac{\Delta v}{a} = \frac{v_1 - v_0}{a}$$
   $$= \frac{0.84 \text{ m/s} - 0.00 \text{ m/s}}{2.0 \times 10^3 \text{ m/s}^2}$$
   $$t = 4.2 \times 10^{-4} \text{ s}$$

8. While descending at a constant speed of 1.0 m/s, a scuba diver releases a cork, which accelerates upward at 3.0 m/s². What is the diver's depth when the cork reaches the surface 2.0 s later?

   $$0 = d_0 + v_0 t + \frac{1}{2}at^2$$
   $$d_0 = d - v_0 t - \frac{1}{2}at^2$$
   $$d_0 = 0.0 \text{ m} - (-1.0 \text{ m/s})(2.0 \text{ s})$$
   $$- \frac{1}{2}(3.0 \text{ m/s}^2)(2.0 \text{ s})^2$$
   $$d_0 = 2.0 \text{ m} - 6.0 \text{ m}$$
   $$d_0 = -4.0 \text{ m}$$
   $$d_{diver} = d_0 + vt = -4.0 \text{ m} + (-1.0 \text{ m/s})(2.0 \text{ s})$$
   $$d_{diver} = -6.0 \text{ m}$$

9. A car with a velocity of +27 m/s slows down at a rate of -8.5 m/s² to a stop in a distance of 43 m on a dry road. The same car traveling at +27 m/s slows down at a rate of -6.5 m/s² to a stop on a wet road.

   a. How much farther does the car travel on the wet road before coming to a stop?

   $$v^2 = v_0^2 + 2a(d - d_0)$$
   $$0 = v_0^2 + 2a(d - 0)$$
   $$d = -\frac{v_0^2}{2a} = -\frac{(27 \text{ m/s})^2}{2(-6.5 \text{ m/s}^2)}$$
   $$d = 56 \text{ m}$$
   $$\Delta d = 56 \text{ m} - 43 \text{ m} = 13 \text{ m}$$

   b. What maximum car speed will allow the car traveling on the wet road to stop in a distance of 43 m?

   $$v^2 = v_0^2 + 2a(d - d_0)$$
   $$0 = v_0^2 + 2a(d - 0)$$
   $$v_0 = \sqrt{-2a(d)} = \sqrt{-2(-6.5 \text{ m/s}^2)(43 \text{ m})}$$
   $$v_0 = +24 \text{ m/s}$$

ANSWER KEY

10. The engine of a toy rocket supplies an average acceleration of 38.0 m/s² to the rocket for an interval of 0.80 s.

   a. If the toy rocket is launched vertically, how high does it rise in this interval?

   $d = d_0 + v_0 t + \frac{1}{2}at^2$

   $= 0.0 \text{ m} + (0.0 \text{ m})(0.80 \text{ s})$
   $+ \frac{1}{2}(38.0 \text{ m/s}^2)(0.80 \text{ s})^2$

   $d = 12 \text{ m}$

   b. How fast is the rocket moving at the end of 0.80 s?

   $v = v_0 + at = (0.0 \text{ m/s}) + (38.0 \text{ m/s}^2)(0.80 \text{ s})$

   $v = 3.0 \times 10^1 \text{ m/s}$

   c. What altitude does the rocket reach before falling back to Earth?

   $d = d_{launch} + d_{freefall}$

   For $d_{freefall}$
   $v^2 = v_0^2 + 2g(d - d_0)$
   $0 = v_0^2 + 2g(d - 0)$
   $d = -\frac{v_0^2}{2a} = -\frac{(3.0 \times 10^1 \text{ m/s})^2}{2(-9.80 \text{ m/s}^2)}$

   $d_{freefall} = 46 \text{ m}$

   $d = 12 \text{ m} + 46 \text{ m}$
   $d = 58 \text{ m}$

   d. How long does it take the rocket to reach this altitude?

   $t = t_{launch} + t_{freefall}$

   For $t_{freefall}$, find the time to fall 46 m from rest. ($d = -46$ m, $d_0 = 0$ m, $v_0 = 0.0$ m/s)

   $d = (0) + 0 + \frac{1}{2}gt^2$

   $t_{freefall} = \sqrt{\frac{2d}{g}} = \sqrt{\frac{2(-46 \text{ m})}{9.80 \text{ m/s}^2}}$

   $t_{freefall} = 3.1 \text{ s}$

   $t = t_{launch} + t_{freefall} = 0.80 \text{ s} + 3.1 \text{ s}$
   $t = 3.9 \text{ s}$

Chapter 6

1. The propellers of a small airplane produce a forward thrust of 6.2×10^4 N on the plane which has a mass of 2.8×10^4 kg. What is the plane's forward acceleration?

   $F = ma$

   $a = \frac{F}{m} = \frac{6.2 \times 10^4 \text{ N}}{2.8 \times 10^4 \text{ kg}}$

   $a = 2.2 \text{ m/s}^2$

2. If the plane in Problem 1 is flying horizontally, what is the lift (upward force of air) on the plane?

   $a_y = 0, F_{net} = 0 = F_{lift} + F_g$
   $F_{lift} = -F_g = -mg$
   $= -(2.8 \times 10^4 \text{ kg})(-9.80 \text{ m/s}^2)$
   $F_{lift} = 2.7 \times 10^5 \text{ N}$

3. A girl in a canoe uses a paddle to push the canoe at rest from a dock giving it a speed of 0.30 m/s. If the paddle is in contact with the dock for 0.75 seconds, what is the average force on the canoe? (The mass of the canoe is 27 kg and that of the girl is 52 kg.)

   $a = \frac{v - v_0}{t} = \frac{0.30 \text{ m/s} - 0.00 \text{ m/s}}{0.75 \text{ s}}$

   $a = 0.40 \text{ m/s}^2$

   $F = ma = (27 \text{ kg} + 52 \text{ kg})(0.40 \text{ m/s}^2)$

   $F = 32 \text{ N}$

4. A student attaches a spring scale to a 2.30-kg book and then releases the book. If the student maintains a scale reading of 25.0 N, what is the magnitude and direction of the book's acceleration? (Assume upward is the positive direction.)

   $F_{net} = F_{spring\ scale} - F_g$
   $= 25.0 \text{ N} - (2.30 \text{ kg})(9.80 \text{ m/s}^2)$
   $F_{net} = 25.0 \text{ N} - 22.5$
   $F_{net} = 2.5 \text{ N}$

   $a = \frac{F}{m} = \frac{2.5 \text{ N}}{2.30 \text{ kg}}$

   $a = 1.1 \text{ m/s}^2$

   The acceleration is 1.1 m/s² upward.

Physics: Principles and Problems

5. If the student in problem 4 maintains a scale reading of 22.0 N, what will be the displacement of the book in 1.0 s?

$F_{net} = F_{spring\ scale} - F_g$
$= 22.0\ N - (2.30\ kg)(9.80\ m/s^2)$
$F_{net} = 22.0\ N - 22.5\ N$
$F_{net} = -0.5\ N$
$a = \dfrac{F}{m} = \dfrac{-0.5\ N}{2.30\ kg}$
$a = -0.2\ m/s^2$
$d = d_0 + v_0 t + \dfrac{1}{2}at^2,\ d_0 = 0\ m,\ v_0 = 0\ m/s$
$d = \dfrac{1}{2}at^2 = \dfrac{1}{2}(-0.2\ m/s^2)(1.0\ s)^2$
$d = -0.1\ m$

6. Two laboratory masses are tied to opposite ends of a weightless string, which passes over a frictionless pulley as shown below.

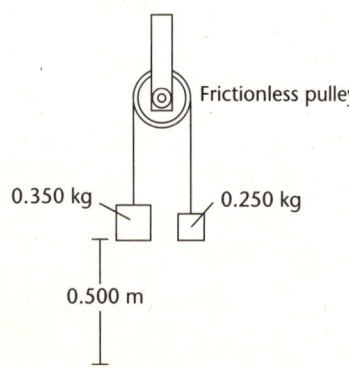

a. If the masses are released from rest, what is the acceleration of the 0.250-kg mass?

$F_{net} = F_{g1} - F_{g2} = m_1 g - m_2 g$
$= (0.350\ kg)(9.00\ m/s^2)$
$\quad - (0.250\ kg)(9.80\ m/s^2)$
$= (0.100\ kg)(9.80\ m/s^2)$
$= 0.980\ N$

$a = \dfrac{F}{m} = \dfrac{0.980\ N}{0.600\ kg}$
$a = 1.63\ m/s^2$, upward

b. After the masses are released, how long will it take the 0.350 kg mass to strike the floor?

$d = d_0 + v_0 t + \dfrac{1}{2}at^2,\ d_0 = 0\ m,$
$v_0 = 0\ m/s$

$d = \dfrac{1}{2}at^2,\ t = \sqrt{\dfrac{2d}{a}}$

$t = \sqrt{\dfrac{2d}{a}} = \sqrt{\dfrac{2(0.500\ m)}{1.63\ m/s^2}}$

$t = 0.783\ s$

c. A student decides to demonstrate this problem. After setting up the equipment, she accurately measures the time it takes the 0.350-kg mass to reach the floor as 0.92 s. If she attributes the cause of the difference in times to the frictional force on the pulley, what is the size of this force?

$d = d_0 + v_0 t + \dfrac{1}{2}at^2,\ d_0 = 0\ m,$
$v_0 = 0\ m/s$

$d = \dfrac{1}{2}at^2$

$a = \dfrac{2d}{t^2} = \dfrac{2(0.500\ m)}{(0.92\ s)^2}$

$a = 1.2\ m/s^2$

$F_{net} = ma = (0.600\ kg)(1.2\ m/s^2)$
$F_{net} = (0.100\ kg)(9.80\ m/s^2) - F_f$
$F_f = 0.980\ N - F_{net} = 0.980\ N - 0.72\ N$
$F_f = 0.26\ N$

ANSWER KEY

7. A horse is pulling two loaded sleds across the snow. The first sled, which has a mass of 250 kg, is attached to the horse by a harness that can withstand a maximum tension of 4500 N. The second sled, which has a mass of 150 kg, is attached to the first sled by a rope that can withstand a maximum tension of 450 N.

   a. What is the acceleration of the sleds just before the rope snaps?

   $T_{2max} = F_2 = m_2 a$

   $a = \dfrac{F_2}{m_2} = \dfrac{450 \text{ N}}{150 \text{ kg}}$

   $a = 3.0 \text{ m/s}^2$

   b. What is the tension in the harness just before the rope snaps?

   $T_1 = F_1 = (m_1 + m_2)a$
   $= (250 \text{ kg} + 150 \text{ kg})3.0 \text{ m/s}^2$

   $T_1 = 1200 \text{ N}$

8. A pendulum with a length of 1.00 m is in a rocket that is far removed from any gravitational effects. If the rocket is accelerating as shown below, what is the period of the pendulum?

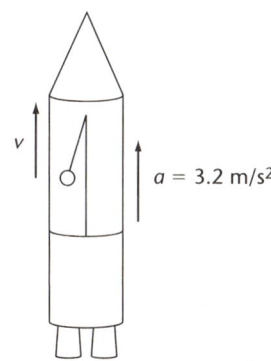

$T = 2\pi \sqrt{\dfrac{l}{a}} = 2\pi \sqrt{\dfrac{1.0 \text{ m}}{3.2 \text{ m/s}^2}}$

$T = 2\pi (0.56 \text{ s})$

$T = 3.5 \text{ s}$

9. A 65.0-kg passenger in a car is securely fastened in a safety belt as shown below.

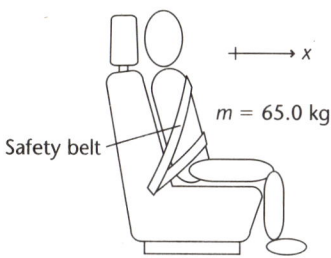

Calculate the magnitude and determine the direction of the horizontal force that the safety belt and seat exert on the passenger for each of the following conditions. (Assume the car is moving only horizontally.)

   a. $v_0 = +20.0$ m/s, $a = 0$ m/s^2

   $F = ma = (65.0 \text{ kg})(0 \text{ m/s}^2)$

   $F = 0 \text{ N}$

   b. $v_0 = +20.0$ m/s, $a = +1.50$ m/s^2

   $F = ma = (65.0 \text{ kg})(+1.50 \text{ m/s}^2)$

   $F = 97.5 \text{ N}$ to the right

   c. $v_0 = 10.0$ m/s, $a = -3.00$ m/s^2

   $F = ma = (65.0 \text{ kg})(-3.00 \text{ m/s}^2)$

   $F = 195 \text{ N}$ to the left

   d. $v_0 = -3.0$ m/s, $a = -1.20$ m/s^2

   $F = ma = (65.0 \text{ kg})(-1.20 \text{ m/s}^2)$

   $F = 78.0 \text{ N}$ to the left

   e. $v_0 = -10.0$ m/s, $a = +2.3$ m/s^2

   $F = ma = (65.0 \text{ kg})(+2.3 \text{ m/s}^2)$

   $F = 1.50 \times 10^2 \text{ N}$ to the right

10. In Problem 9, the car is traveling at 20.0 m/s and the driver suddenly slows down the car at a rate of 5.00 m/s^2.

    a. What is the magnitude and direction of the force that the passenger exerts on the safety belt and seat?

    $F_{\text{passenger on safety belt and seat}}$
    $= -F_{\text{safety belt and seat on passenger}}$
    $= -ma = -(65.0 \text{ kg})(-5.00 \text{ m/s}^2)$

    $F_{\text{passenger on safety belt and seat}}$
    $= 325 \text{ N}$ to the right

b. After slowing down, the driver accelerates the car forward at a rate of 1.50 m/s². What is the magnitude and direction of the force that the passenger exerts on the safety belt and seat?

$F_{\text{passenger on safety belt and seat}}$
$= -F_{\text{safety belt and seat on passenger}}$
$= -ma = -(65.0 \text{ kg})(+1.50 \text{ m/s}^2)$

$F_{\text{passenger on safety belt and seat}} = -97.5 \text{ N}$

$F_{\text{passenger on safety belt and seat}} = 97.5 \text{ N to the left}$

Chapter 7

1. A dog tugs forward with force of 28 N on a taut leash at an angle of 15° from the horizontal. What is the magnitude of the tension in the leash?

$T_y = T\cos\theta = F_p$

$T = \dfrac{F_p}{\cos\theta} = \dfrac{28 \text{ N}}{\cos(15°)}$

$T = 29 \text{ N}$

2. A rod supports a 2.35-kg lamp as shown below.

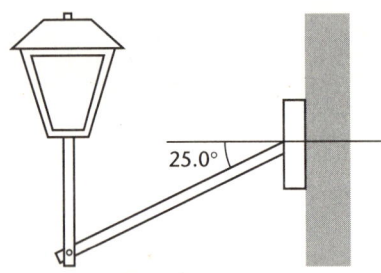

 a. What is the magnitude of the tension in the rod?

$T_y = T\sin\theta = mg$

$T = \dfrac{mg}{\sin\theta} = \dfrac{(2.35 \text{ kg})(9.80 \text{ m/s}^2)}{\sin(25.0°)}$

$T = 54.4 \text{ N}$

 b. Calculate the components of the force that the bracket exerts on the rod?

$F_x = T_x = T\cos\theta = (54.4 \text{ N})\cos(25.0°)$

$F_x = 49.3 \text{ N, outward}$

$F_y = T_y = mg = (2.35 \text{ kg})(9.80 \text{ m/s}^2)$
$= 23.0 \text{ N, upward}$

3. A 20.0-N box is resting on a frictionless surface as shown below.

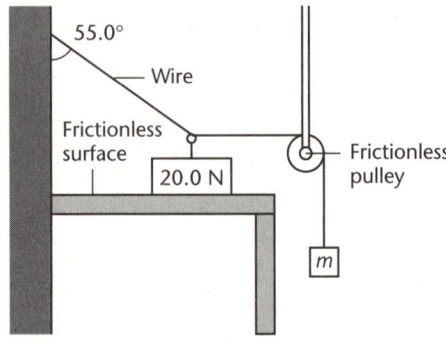

 a. If the magnitude of the tension in the wire is 12.0 N, what is the value of the mass, m?

$T\cos\theta = F_p = mg$

$m = \dfrac{T\cos\theta}{g} = \dfrac{12.0 \text{ N} \cos(35.0°)}{9.80 \text{ m/s}^2}$

$m = 1.00 \text{ kg}$

 b. The table supporting the box is removed and the height of the pulley is adjusted so that the string connecting mass, m, and the box remains parallel to the floor. What is the magnitude and orientation of the tension in the wire?

$T\cos\theta = mg = (1.00 \text{ kg})(9.80 \text{ m/s}^2)$
$= 9.80 \text{ N}$

$T\sin\theta = 20.0 \text{ N}$

$T = \dfrac{9.80 \text{ N}}{\cos\theta}; \ T = \dfrac{20.0 \text{ N}}{\sin\theta}$

$\dfrac{\sin\theta}{\cos\theta} = \tan\theta = \dfrac{20.0 \text{ N}}{9.80 \text{ N}} = 2.04$

$\theta = \tan^{-1}(2.04) = 64.0°$

$T = \dfrac{9.80 \text{ N}}{\cos\theta} = \dfrac{9.80 \text{ N}}{\cos(64.0°)}$

$T = 22.4 \text{ N at 116°}$

4. A 25.0-kg crate has an adjustable handle so that it can be pushed or pulled by the handle at various angles.

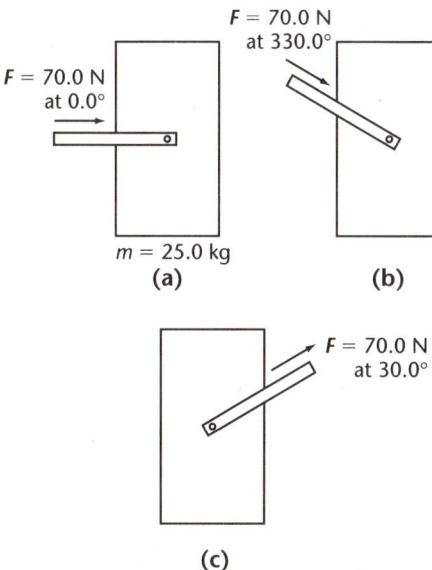

Determine the acceleration of the crate for each situation shown in the diagram knowing that the coefficient of sliding friction between the floor and the bottom of the crate is 0.20.

For (a)

y-direction: $F_N = F_g = mg$; $F_N = mg$

x-direction: $F_p - F_f = ma$

$F_f = \mu_k F_N = \mu_k mg$

$a = \dfrac{F_{net}}{m} = \dfrac{F_p - \mu_k mg}{m} = \dfrac{F_p}{m} - \mu_k g$

$a = \dfrac{70.0 \text{ N}}{25.0 \text{ kg}} - (0.20)(9.80 \text{ m/s}^2)$

$a = 0.84 \text{ m/s}^2$

For (b)

y-direction: $F_N = F_g + F_y$
$= mg + F \sin(30.0°)$

x-direction: $F_p = F \cos(30.0°)$;
$F \cos(30.0°) - F_f = ma$

$F_f = \mu_k F_N = \mu_k(mg + F \sin(30.0°))$

$a = \dfrac{F_{net}}{m}$

$= \dfrac{F_p \cos(30.0°) - \mu_k(mg + F \sin(30.0°))}{m}$

$a = \dfrac{F_p(\cos(30.0°) - \mu_k \sin(30.0°))}{m} - \mu_k g$

$a = \dfrac{70.0 \text{ N }(0.8660) - (0.20)(0.5000)}{25.0 \text{ kg}}$
$- (.20)(9.80 \text{ m/s}^2)$

$a = 0.18 \text{ m/s}^2$

For (c)

y-direction: $F_N = F_g - F_y$
$= mg - F \sin(30.0°)$

x-direction: $F_p = F \cos(30.0°)$;
$F \cos(30.0°) - F_f = ma$

$F_f = \mu_k F_N = \mu_k(mg - F \sin(30.0°))$

$a = \dfrac{F_{net}}{m}$

$= \dfrac{F_p \cos(30.0°) - \mu_k(mg - F \sin(30.0°))}{m}$

$a = \dfrac{F_p(\cos(30.0°) + \mu_k \sin(30.0°))}{m} - \mu_k g$

$a = \dfrac{70.0 \text{N }(0.8660) - (0.20)(0.5000)}{25.0 \text{ kg}}$
$- (.20)(9.80 \text{ m/s}^2)$

$a = 0.35 \text{ m/s}^2$

5. A child shoves a small toboggan weighing 100.0-N up a snowy hill, giving the toboggan an initial speed of 6.0 m/s. If the hill is inclined at an angle of 32° above the horizontal, how far along the hill will the toboggan slide? Assume the coefficient of sliding friction between the toboggan and the snow is 0.15.

y-direction

$F_{net, y} = ma_y = 0$

$F_N - F_{gy} = 0$

$F_N = F_{gy} = mg \cos \theta$

$F_p = F_f = \mu_k F_N = \mu_k F_g \cos \theta$

x-direction

$F_{net, xy} = ma_x = ma$

$F_{gx} - F_f = ma$

$ma = mg \sin \theta - \mu_k F_N$

$ma = mg \sin \theta - \mu_k mg \cos \theta$

$a = g(\sin\theta - \mu_k\cos\theta)$
$= 9.80 \text{ m/s}^2(\sin 32° - 0.15 \cos 32°)$
$a = 3.9 \text{ m/s}^2$

$v^2 = v_0^2 + 2a(d - d_0)^2$

$0 = v_0^2 + 2ad^2$

$d = -\sqrt{\dfrac{v_0^2}{2a}} = -\sqrt{\dfrac{(-6.0 \text{ m/s})^2}{2(3.9 \text{ m/s}^2)}} = -2.1 \text{ m}$

$d = 2.1$ m, up the hill

6. A nozzle in a fountain is angled 23° below the horizontal and is located 2.0 m above the edge of the basin. If the water is ejected at a speed of 4.2 m/s from the nozzle, how far from the edge of the basin does the water fall?

y-direction

$v_y = v \sin\theta = (4.2 \text{ m/s})\sin(23°)$
$v_y = 1.6 \text{ m/s}$

$y = y_0 + v_{y0}t - \dfrac{1}{2}gt^2$

$0 \text{ m} = 2 \text{ m} + (-1.6 \text{ m/s})t - \dfrac{1}{2}(9.80 \text{ m/s}^2)t^2$

$0 \text{ m} = 2 \text{ m} + (-1.6 \text{ m/s})t - (4.9 \text{ m/s}^2)t^2$

Solving the quadratic equation in the form $ax^2 + bx + c = 0$,

for $a = (-4.9)$, $b = (-1.6)$ and $c = 2$, yields

$x = 0.50$

Therefore, $t = 0.50$ s

x-direction

$v_x = v \cos\theta = (4.2 \text{ m/s})\cos(23°)$
$v_x = 3.9 \text{ m/s}$

$x = x_0 + v_{x0}t = 0.0 \text{ m} + (3.9 \text{ m/s})(0.50 \text{ s})$
$x = 2.0 \text{ m}$

7. A juggler tosses a ball from his right hand to his left hand, which is at the same level as his right hand and 0.60 m to the side. If the ball reaches a height of 0.80 m above the level of his hands, with what velocity does the ball leave his right hand?

y-direction

$y = y_0 + v_{y0}t - \dfrac{1}{2}gt^2$

at $d_{y0} = 0.80$ m, $d_y = 0$ m, $v_{y0} = 0$ m/s

$0 = d_{y0} - \dfrac{1}{2}gt^2$

$t = \sqrt{\dfrac{2y_0}{g}} = \sqrt{\dfrac{2(0.80 \text{ m})}{9.8 \text{ m/s}^2}}$

$t = 0.40$ s

At $t = 0.40$ s, $v_y = 0$

$0 = v_{y0} + gt$

$v_{y0} = -gt = (-9.80 \text{ m/s}^2)(0.40 \text{ s})$

$v_{y0} = 3.9$ m/s

x-direction

at landing, $y = 0$,

$0 = 0 + v_{y0}t - \dfrac{1}{2}gt^2$

$t = \dfrac{2v_{y0}}{g} = \dfrac{2(3.9 \text{ m/s})}{9.8 \text{ m/s}^2}$

$t = 0.80$ s

$R = v_{x0}t$

$v_{x0} = \dfrac{R}{t} = \dfrac{0.60 \text{ m}}{0.80 \text{ s}}$

$v_{x0} = 0.75$ m/s

$v = \sqrt{v_{x0}^2 + v_{y0}^2}$
$= \sqrt{(3.9 \text{ m/s})^2 + (0.75 \text{ m/s})^2}$

$v = 4.0$ m/s

$\tan\theta = \dfrac{v_{y0}}{v_{x0}} = \dfrac{3.9 \text{ m/s}}{0.75 \text{ m/s}}$

$\tan\theta = 5.2$

$\theta = \tan^{-1}(5.2) = 79°$

$v = 4.0$ m/s at 79°

8. A skateboarder is slowing down at a rate of 0.70 m/s². At the moment he is moving 1.5 m/s forward, he throws a basketball upward a distance of 3.0 m and catches it at the same level it was thrown without changing his position on the skateboard. Determine the vertical and horizontal components of the ball's velocity relative to the skateboard when the ball left his hand.

y-direction

$$y = y_0 + v_{y0}t - \frac{1}{2}gt^2$$

$$v_y^2 = v_{y0}^2 - 2g(y - y_0)$$

at its highest position, $v_y = 0$, $y_0 = 0$

$$0 = v_{y0}^2 - 2g(y)$$

$$v_{y0} = \sqrt{2gy} = \sqrt{2(9.80 \text{ m/s}^2)(3.0 \text{ m})}$$

$$v_{y0} = 7.7 \text{ m/s}$$

falling from its highest point, $v_{y0} = 0$

$$y = 0 + 0 - \frac{1}{2}gt_{down}^2$$

$$t_{down} = \sqrt{\frac{-2y}{g}} = \sqrt{\frac{-2(-3.0 \text{ m})}{9.8 \text{ m/s}^2}}$$

$$t_{down} = 0.78 \text{ s}$$

$$t = 2t_{down} = 2(0.78 \text{ s})$$

$$t = 1.6 \text{ s}$$

x-direction

distance skateboard moves

$$x_s = x_{s0} + v_{s0}t + \frac{1}{2}at^2$$

$$= 0 + (1.5 \text{ m/s})(1.6 \text{ s})$$

$$+ \frac{1}{2}(-0.70 \text{ m/s}^2)(1.6 \text{ s})^2$$

$$x_1 = 1.5 \text{ m}$$

distance vertically thrown ball moves

$$x_2 = v_b t = (1.5 \text{ m/s})(1.6 \text{ s})$$

$$x_2 = 2.4 \text{ m}$$

$$x_2 + \Delta x = x_1,$$

distance skateboard lags behind ball

$$\Delta x = x_1 - x_2 = 1.5 \text{ m} - 2.4 \text{ m}$$

$$\Delta x = -0.9 \text{ m}$$

Horizontal velocity skateboarder must throw ball relative to skateboard

$$v_{x0} = \Delta x/t = (-0.9 \text{ m})/(1.6 \text{ s})$$

$$v_{x0} = -0.6 \text{ m/s}$$

$$v_{x0} = 0.6 \text{ m/s opposite the direction of motion}$$

9. The beaters of an electric mixer are shown below.

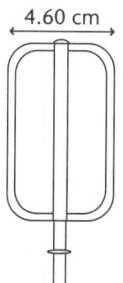

4.60 cm

What is the acceleration of the outer part of a blade as it rotates at a rate of 1200 revolutions per minute?

$$T = \left(\frac{60 \text{ s}}{1 \text{ min}}\right)\left(\frac{1 \text{ min}}{1200 \text{ revolutions}}\right)$$

$$= 5.0 \times 10^{-2} \text{ s}$$

$$a = \frac{4\pi^2 r}{T^2}$$

$$= \frac{4\pi^2(2.30 \times 10^{-2} \text{ m})}{(5.0 \times 10^{-2} \text{ s})^2}$$

$$a = 360 \text{ m/s}^2$$

10. A clown rides a small car at a speed of 15 km/h along a circular path with a radius of 3.5 m.

   a. What is the magnitude of the centripetal force on a 0.18-kg ball held by the clown?

$$v = \left(\frac{15 \text{ km}}{\text{h}}\right)\left(\frac{1000 \text{ m}}{1 \text{ km}}\right)\left(\frac{1 \text{ h}}{3600 \text{ s}}\right)$$

$$v = 4.2 \text{ m/s}$$

$$F_c = ma_c = m\frac{v^2}{r} = (0.18 \text{ kg})\frac{(4.2 \text{ m/s})^2}{3.5 \text{ m}}$$

$$F_c = 0.91 \text{ N}$$

Physics: Principles and Problems

Supplemental Problems Answer Key **81**

b. At the point where the car is headed due north, the clown throws the ball vertically upward with a speed of 5.0 m/s relative to the moving car. To where must a second clown run to catch the ball the same distance above the ground as it was thrown?

y-direction

Time to reach highest point

$v_y = v_{y0} - gt$

When $v_y = 0$, $t = \dfrac{v_{y0}}{g}$

$t = \dfrac{5.0 \text{ m/s}}{9.80 \text{ m/s}^2}$

$t = 0.51$ s

Total time ball is in air is twice the time needed to reach the highest point.

$t_{total} = 2(0.51 \text{ s}) = 1.0$ s

x-direction

$R = v_{x0}t = (4.2 \text{ m/s})(1.0 \text{ s})$

$R = 4.2$ m north of the point where the clown threw the ball.

Chapter 8

1. The satellites of Mars, Phobos and Deimos, have mean orbital radii of 9.38×10^6 m and 2.35×10^7 m, respectively. The orbital period of Deimos is 30.30 hr. Use Kepler's third law of planetary motion to predict the period of Phobos.

$\left(\dfrac{T_{Phobos}}{T_{Deimos}}\right)^2 = \left(\dfrac{r_{Phobos}}{r_{Deimos}}\right)^3$

$T_{Phobos} = T_{Deimos} \sqrt{\left(\dfrac{r_{Phobos}}{r_{Deimos}}\right)^3} = (30.30 \text{ h}) \sqrt{\left(\dfrac{9.38 \times 10^6 \text{ m}}{2.35 \times 10^7 \text{ m}}\right)^3}$

$T_{Phobos} = 7.64$ h

2. Use Kepler's third law to predict the altitude of a Martian satellite that would have a period of 24.0 h.

$\left(\dfrac{T_s}{T_{Deimos}}\right)^2 = \left(\dfrac{r_s}{r_{Deimos}}\right)^3$

$r_s = (r_{Deimos}) \sqrt[3]{\left(\dfrac{T_s}{T_{Deimos}}\right)^2} = (2.35 \times 10^7 \text{ m}) \sqrt[3]{\left(\dfrac{24.0 \text{ h}}{30.30 \text{ h}}\right)^2}$

$r_s = 2.01 \times 10^7$ m

$a_s = r_s - r_{Mars} = 2.01 \times 10^7 \text{ m} - 3.40 \times 10^6 \text{ m}$

$a_s = 1.67 \times 10^7$ m

ANSWER KEY

3. Use Newton's form of Kepler's third law and the information about Deimos in Problem 1 to determine the mass of Mars.

$$T^2_{Deimos} = \left(\frac{4\pi^2}{Gm_{Mars}}\right) r^3_{Deimos}$$

$$m_{Mars} = \left(\frac{4\pi^2}{GT^2_{Deimos}}\right) r^3_{Deimos}$$

$$= \left(\frac{4\pi^2}{6.67 \times 10^{-11} \text{ N·m}^2/\text{kg}^2[(30.30 \text{ h})(3600 \text{ s/h})]^2}\right)(2.35 \times 10^7 \text{ m})^3$$

$$m_{Mars} = 6.45 \times 10^{23} \text{ kg}$$

4. The Martian moon, *Deimos*, has a mass of 2.4×10^{15} kg and an average radius of 6.4 km. What is the acceleration of gravity at its surface?

$$g_{Deimos} = \frac{Gm_{Deimos}}{r^2_{Deimos}}$$

$$= \left(\frac{6.67 \times 10^{-11} \text{ N·m}^2/\text{kg}^2(2.4 \times 10^{15} \text{ kg})}{(6.4 \times 10^3 \text{ m})^2}\right)$$

$$g_{Deimos} = 3.9 \times 10^{-3} \text{ m/s}^2$$

5. What is the gravitational attraction between two protons ($m_{proton} = 1.67 \times 10^{-27}$ kg) at a distance of 5.0×10^{-15} m, about the diameter of the nucleus of an atom?

$$F_g = \frac{Gm_1 m_2}{d^2} = \frac{(6.67 \times 10^{-11} \text{ N·m}^2/\text{kg}^2)(1.67 \times 10^{-27} \text{ kg})(1.67 \times 10^{-27} \text{ kg})}{(5.0 \times 10^{-15} \text{ m})^2}$$

$$F_g = 7.4 \times 10^{-36} \text{ N}$$

6. Two bowling balls, each with a mass of 6.80 kg, are 1.00 m apart. Compare the weight of the first ball with the gravitational force exerted on it by the second ball.

$$F_g = mg = (6.80 \text{ kg})(9.80 \text{ m/s}^2)$$

$$F_{g1} = 66.6 \text{ N}$$

$$F_g = \frac{Gm_1 m_2}{d^2} = \frac{(6.67 \times 10^{-11} \text{ N·m}^2/\text{kg}^2)(6.80 \text{ kg})(6.80 \text{ kg})}{(1.0 \text{ m})^2}$$

$$F_{g2} = 3.08 \times 10^{-9} \text{ N}$$

$$\frac{F_{g1}}{F_{g2}} = \frac{66.6 \text{ N}}{3.08 \times 10^{-9} \text{ N}} = 2.16 \times 10^{10}$$

7. Saturn's rings are made of particles moving in orbits around the planet. The inner edge of the closest ring has a radius of 6.7×10^4 km while the radius of the outer edge of the farthest ring is 4.8×10^5 km. The mass of Saturn is 5.69×10^{26} kg.

   a. Calculate the velocity of a particle near the inner edge of the closest ring.

$$v = \sqrt{\frac{Gm_{Saturn}}{r}} = \sqrt{\frac{(6.67 \times 10^{-11} \text{ N·m}^2/\text{kg}^2)(5.69 \times 10^{26} \text{ kg})}{6.7 \times 10^7 \text{ m}}}$$

$$v = 2.4 \times 10^4 \text{ m/s}$$

Physics: Principles and Problems

b. What is the period of this particle?

$$T = 2\pi\sqrt{\frac{r^3}{Gm_{Saturn}}} = 2\pi\sqrt{\frac{(6.7 \times 10^7 \text{ m})^3}{(6.67 \times 10^{-11} \text{ N·m}^2/\text{kg}^2)(5.69 \times 10^{26} \text{ kg})}}$$

$T = 1.8 \times 10^4$ s

c. How do the answers of 6a and 6b compare to the velocity and period of a particle orbiting near the outer edge of the farthest ring?

$$\frac{v_1}{v_2} = \frac{\sqrt{\frac{Gm_{Saturn}}{r_1}}}{\sqrt{\frac{Gm_{Saturn}}{r_2}}} = \sqrt{\frac{r_2}{r_1}} = \sqrt{\frac{4.8 \times 10^8 \text{ m}}{6.7 \times 10^7 \text{ m}}}$$

$$\frac{v_1}{v_2} = 2.7$$

$$\frac{T_1}{T_2} = \frac{2\pi\sqrt{\frac{r_1^3}{Gm_{Saturn}}}}{2\pi\sqrt{\frac{r_2^3}{Gm_{Saturn}}}} = \sqrt{\frac{r_1^3}{r_2^3}} = \sqrt{\frac{(6.7 \times 10^7 \text{ m})^3}{(4.8 \times 10^8 \text{ m})^3}}$$

$$\frac{T_1}{T_2} = 5.2 \times 10^{-2}$$

8. The mass of the moon is 7.34×10^{22} kg and its average radius is 1785 km.

a. Between January, 1998, and December, 1998, the *Lunar Prospector* was in a nearly circular orbit around the moon at an altitude of 1.0×10^2 km. What was the period of the *Lunar Prospector* in minutes?

$$T = 2\pi\sqrt{\frac{r^3}{Gm_{Moon}}} = 2\pi\sqrt{\frac{(1.885 \times 10^6 \text{ m})^3}{(6.67 \times 10^{-11} \text{ N·m}^2/\text{kg}^2)(7.34 \times 10^{22} \text{ kg})}}$$

$T = (7.35 \times 10^3 \text{ s})(1 \text{ min}/60 \text{ s})$

$T = 123$ min

b. What was its velocity when it was in the orbit at 1.0×10^2 km?

$$v = \sqrt{\frac{Gm_{Moon}}{r}} = \sqrt{\frac{(6.67 \times 10^{-11} \text{ N·m}^2/\text{kg}^2)(7.34 \times 10^{22} \text{ kg})}{1.885 \times 10^6 \text{ m}}}$$

$v = 1.61 \times 10^3$ m/s

ANSWER KEY

9. At the moon's surface g_{Moon} has a value of 1.59 m/s². What is the value of the acceleration of gravity at an altitude of 1.00×10^2 km above the moon's surface?

$$a = g_{Moon}\left(\frac{r_{Moon}}{d}\right)^2 = 1.59 \text{ m/s}^2 \left(\frac{1.785 \times 10^6 \text{ m}}{1.785 \times 10^6 \text{ m} + 1.00 \times 10^5 \text{ m}}\right)^2$$

$a = 1.43$ m/s²

10. Use Table 8-1 in the text to find the sun's gravitational field strength at Earth's orbit.

$$g = \sqrt{\frac{Gm_s}{d}} = \sqrt{\frac{(6.67 \times 10^{-11} \text{ N·m}^2/\text{kg}^2)(1.99 \times 10^{30} \text{ kg})}{(1.50 \times 10^{11} \text{ m})^2}}$$

$g = 7.68 \times 10^{-2}$ m/s²

Chapter 9

1. A 26.0-g arrow leaves a bowstring at a velocity of +46 m/s.

   a. What is the impulse on the arrow?

   $F\Delta t = m\Delta v = mv_2 - mv_1 = m(v_2 - 0)$
   $= (0.026 \text{ kg})(46 \text{ m/s}) = 1.2$ kg·m/s

   $F\Delta t = 1.2$ kg·m/s

   b. What is the average force that the string exerts on the arrow if the string is in contact with the arrow for 6.0×10^{-3} s?

   $F\Delta t = 1.2$ kg·m/s

   $$F = \frac{1.2 \text{ kg·m/s}}{\Delta t} = \frac{1.2 \text{ kg·m/s}}{6.0 \times 10^{-3} \text{ s}}$$

   $F = 2.0 \times 10^2$ N

   c. What average force does the arrow exert on the string during this interval?

   $F_{1,2} = -F_{2,1} = -2.0 \times 10^2$ N

2. The *v-t* graph below shows the velocity changes of a 0.145-kg baseball as it is caught by player A and then by player B.

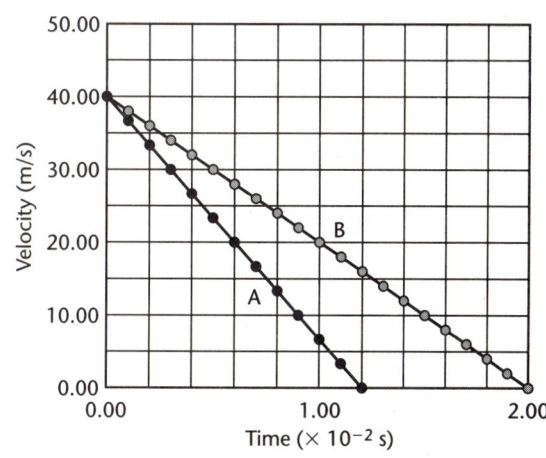

ANSWER KEY

a. Plot an *F-t* graph showing the impulse each player exerts on the ball.

$F\Delta t = m\Delta v = mv^2 - mv^1$
$= m(0 - v_2) = -mv_2$

$F_A = \dfrac{-mv_2}{\Delta t} = \dfrac{-(0.145 \text{ kg})(40.0 \text{ m/s})}{1.20 \times 10^{-3} \text{ s}}$

$F_A = -4830 \text{ N}$

$F_B = \dfrac{-mv_2}{\Delta t} = \dfrac{-(0.145 \text{ kg})(40.0 \text{ m/s})}{2.00 \times 10^{-3} \text{ s}}$

$F_B = -2.90 \times 10^3 \text{ N}$

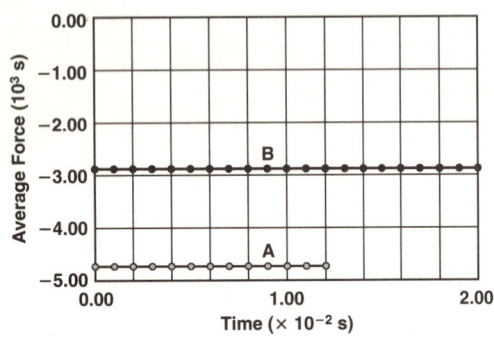

b. Explain which player more likely pulled back (moved in the direction of the ball) his glove while catching the ball.

Because Δt was greater for Player B, this indicates that Player B pulled back while catching the ball.

3. After dropping from a height 1.50 m onto a concrete floor, a 50.0-g ball rebounds to a height of 0.90 m.

a. Find the impulse acting on the ball as it dropped.

$v^2 = v_0^2 - 2g(d - d_0) = 2gd$
$v = \sqrt{-2gd} = \sqrt{2(9.80 \text{ m/s}^2)(1.50 \text{ m})}$
$v = -5.4 \text{ m/s}$
$\Delta v = v - v_0 = -5.4 \text{ m/s} - 0 \text{ m/s}$
$\Delta v = -5.4 \text{ m/s}$
$F\Delta t = m\Delta v = (0.050 \text{ kg})(-5.4 \text{ m/s})$
$F\Delta t = -0.27 \text{ N·s}$

b. Find the impulse acting on the ball on its rebound.

$0 = v_0^2 - 2g(d - d_0) = v_0^2 - 2gd$
$v_0 = \sqrt{2gd} = \sqrt{2(9.80 \text{ m/s}^2)(0.90 \text{ m})}$

$v_0 = 4.2 \text{ m/s}$
$\Delta v = v - v_0 = 0.0 \text{ m/s} - 4.2 \text{ m/s}$
$\Delta v = -4.2 \text{ m/s}$
$F\Delta t = m\Delta v = (0.050 \text{ kg})(-4.2 \text{ m/s})$
$F\Delta t = -0.21 \text{ N·s}$

c. Find the impulse on the ball while it was in contact with the floor.

$\Delta v = v - v_0 = 4.2 \text{ m} - -5.4 \text{ m/s}$
$\Delta v = v - v_0 = 9.6 \text{ m/s}$
$F\Delta t = m\Delta v = (0.050 \text{ kg})(9.6 \text{ m/s})$
$F\Delta t = 0.48 \text{ N·s}$

4. A 180-kg crate is sitting on the flatbed of a moving truck. The coefficient of sliding friction between the crate and the truck bed is 0.30. Two taut cables are attached to either side of the crate. Each cable can exert a maximum horizontal force of 650 N either forward or backward if the crate begins to slide. If the truck stops in 1.8 s, what is the maximum speed the truck could have been moving without breaking the cables?

$F_N = mg$
$F_f = \mu_s F_N = \mu_k mg$
$F\Delta t = m\Delta v$
$(F_f + 2F)\Delta t = m(v - 0)$
$v = \dfrac{(F_f + 2F)\Delta t}{m} = \left(\mu_k g + \dfrac{2F}{m}\right)\Delta t$
$v = \left((0.30)(9.80 \text{ m/s}^2) + \dfrac{2(650 \text{ N})}{180 \text{ kg}}\right)(1.8 \text{ s})$
$v = 18 \text{ m/s}$

5. A single uranium atom has a mass of 3.97×10^{-25} kg. It decays into the nucleus of a thorium atom by emitting an alpha particle at a speed of 2.10×10^7 m/s. The mass of an alpha particle is 6.68×10^{-27} kg. What is the recoil speed of the thorium nucleus?

$p_{A2} + p_{B2} = p_{A1} + p_{B2}$
$m_{alpha}v_{alpha} + m_{thorium}v_{thorium}$
$= m_{uranium}v_{uranium}$
$m_{thorium} + m_{alpha} = m_{uranium}$

86 *Supplemental Problems Answer Key*

ANSWER KEY

$v_{uranium} = 0$

$v_{thorium} = -\dfrac{m_{alpha}v_{alpha}}{m_{thorium}}$

$= -\dfrac{m_{alpha}v_{alpha}}{m_{uranium} - m_{alpha}}$

$= -\dfrac{(6.68 \times 10^{-27}\text{ kg})(2.10 \times 10^7\text{ m/s})}{3.97 \times 10^{-25}\text{ kg} - 0.06 \times 10^{-25}\text{ kg}}$

$v_{thorium} = -3.59 \times 10^5$ m/s

6. A 62-kg boy on a 1.50-kg skateboard moving at $+1.2$ m/s steps off and lands on the sidewalk with a velocity of $+1.1$ m/s. How fast is the skateboard moving?

$p_{A2} + p_{B2} = p_{A1} + p_{B2}$

$m_{boy}v_{boy2} + m_{board}v_{board2} = (m_{boy} + m_{board})v_1$

$v_{board2} = \dfrac{(m_{boy} + m_{board})v_1 - m_{boy}v_{boy2}}{m_{board}} = \dfrac{(62\text{ kg} + 1.5\text{ kg})(1.2\text{ m/s}) - (62\text{ kg})(1.1\text{ m/s})}{1.5\text{ kg}}$

$v_{board2} = +5.3$ m/s

7. A 60.0-kg girl with two 4.0-kg bricks is sitting on frictionless ice. She throws both bricks at the same time forward at a velocity of 6.00 m/s relative to her. What is the velocity of the girl?

$p_{A2} + p_{B2} = p_{A1} + p_{B2}$

$m_{girl}v_{girl2} + 2m_{brick}v_{brick2} = (m_{girl} + m_{brick})v_1$

$m_{girl}v_{girl2} + 2m_{brick}v_{brick2} = 0$

$v_{girl2} = -\dfrac{2m_{brick}v_{brick2}}{m_{girl}} = -\dfrac{2(4.0\text{ kg})(6.00\text{ m/s})}{60.0\text{ kg}}$

$v_{girl2} = -0.80$ m/s

8. The girl in Problem 7 throws one brick and then the other each with a velocity of 6.00 m/s relative to her. What is the velocity of the girl after she throws the second brick?

After the first throw

$(m_{girl} + m_{brick})v_2 + m_{brick}v_{brick2} = (m_{girl} + m_{brick})v_1$

$(m_{girl} + m_{brick})v_2 + m_{brick}v_{brick2} = 0$

$v_2 = -\dfrac{m_{brick}v_{brick2}}{(m_{girl} + m_{brick})} = -\dfrac{(4.0\text{ kg})(6.00\text{ m/s})}{62.0\text{ kg}}$

$v_2 = -0.39$ m/s

For second throw,

$m_{girl}v_{girl2} + m_{brick}v_{brick2} = (m_{girl} + m_{brick})v_2$

$v_{girl2} = \dfrac{(m_{girl} + m_{brick})v_2 - m_{brick}v_{brick2}}{m_{girl}}$

$v_{book\ relative\ to\ ground} = v_{book\ relative\ to\ girl} + v_{girl\ relative\ to\ ground}$

$v_{brick2} = 6.00$ m/s $- 0.39$ m/s $= 5.61$ m/s

$$v_{girl2} = \frac{(60.0 \text{ kg} + 2.0 \text{ kg})(-0.39 \text{ m/s}) - (4.0 \text{ kg})(5.61 \text{ m/s})}{60.0 \text{ kg}}$$

$v_{girl2} = -0.77$ m/s

9. A boy and a dog are standing on a 110-kg diving raft in the middle of a lake. Just as the 55-kg boy dives off the raft with a horizontal velocity of 4.0 m/s due east, the 22-kg dog leaps off the raft horizontally with a velocity of 5.0 m/s due north. What is the resulting velocity of the raft?

$p_2 = p_1 = 0$

$p_2 = p_{Boy2} + p_{Dog2} + p_{Raft2} = 0$

$p_{Raft2} = -(p_{Boy2} + p_{Dog2})$

$(p_{Boy2} + p_{Dog2}) = p_{Boy2,Dog2}$

$p_{Boy2,Dog2} = \sqrt{p_{Boy2}^2 + p_{Dog2}^2} = \sqrt{(m_{Boy}v_{Boy2})^2 + (m_{Dog}v_{Dog2})^2}$

$= \sqrt{((55 \text{ kg})(4.0 \text{ m/s}))^2 + ((22 \text{ kg})(5.0 \text{ m/s}))^2}$

$p_{Boy2,Dog2} = 250$ kg·m/s

$\tan\theta = \frac{p_{Boy2}}{p_{Dog2}} = \frac{(55 \text{ kg})(4.0 \text{ m/s})}{(22 \text{ kg})(5.0 \text{ m/s})} = 2.0$

$\theta = \tan^{-1}(2.0) = 63°$, north of east

$p_{Raft2} = 250$ kg·m/s, 63°, south of west

$v_{Raft2} = \frac{p_{Raft2}}{m_{Raft}} = \frac{(250 \text{ kg·m/s})}{(110 \text{ kg})}$

$v_{Raft2} = 2.3$ m/s, 63°, south of west

10. A 2.00-kg puck moving to the right at a velocity of 6.00 m/s at an angle of 45.0° below the horizontal collides at point A with a 1.00-kg puck traveling to the right at a velocity of 3.00 m/s at an angle of 45.0° above the horizontal as shown below.

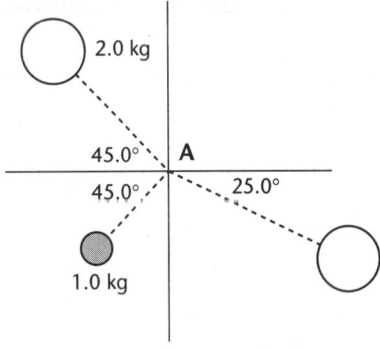

After the collision the 2.0-kg puck moves toward the right a velocity of 4.50 m/s at an angle of 25.0° below the horizontal. What is the velocity of the 1.0-kg puck immediately after the collision?

$p_{A2} + p_{B2} = p_{A1} + p_{B1}$

y-direction

$p_{A2y} + p_{B2y} = p_{A1y} + p_{A2y}$

$p_{B2y} = p_{A1y} + p_{B1y} - p_{A2y}$

$v_{B2y} = \dfrac{m_A v_{A1y} + m_A v_{B1y} - m_A v_{A2y}}{m_B}$

$m_A v_{A1y} = (2.00 \text{ kg})(6.00 \text{ m/s})\sin(45.0°) = 8.48 \text{ kg·m/s}$

$m_B v_{B1y} = (1.00 \text{ kg})(3.00 \text{ m/s})\sin(45.0°) = 2.12 \text{ kg·m/s}$

$m_A v_{A2y} = (2.00 \text{ kg})(4.00 \text{ m/s})\sin(25.0°) = 3.38 \text{ kg·m/s}$

$v_{B2y} = \dfrac{-8.48 \text{ kg·m/s} + 2.12 \text{ kg·m/s} - (-3.38 \text{ kg·m/s})}{1.00 \text{ kg}}$

$v_{B2y} = -2.98 \text{ m/s}$

x-direction

$p_{A2x} + p_{B2x} = p_{A1x} + p_{A2x}$

$p_{B2x} = p_{A1x} + p_{B1x} - p_{A2x}$

$v_{B2x} = \dfrac{m_A v_{A1x} + m_A v_{B1x} - m_A v_{A2x}}{m_B}$

$m_A v_{A1x} = (2.00 \text{ kg})(6.00 \text{ m/s})\cos(45.0°) = 8.48 \text{ kg·m/s}$

$m_B v_{B1x} = (1.00 \text{ kg})(3.00 \text{ m/s})\cos(45.0°) = 2.12 \text{ kg·m/s}$

$m_A v_{A2x} = (2.00 \text{ kg})(4.50 \text{ m/s})\cos(25.0°) = 8.15 \text{ kg·m/s}$

$v_{B2x} = \dfrac{8.48 \text{ kg·m/s} + 2.12 \text{ kg·m/s} - (8.15 \text{ kg·m/s})}{1.00 \text{ kg}}$

$v_{B2x} = 2.45 \text{ m/s}$

$v_{B2} = \sqrt{v_{B2x}^2 + v_{B2y}^2} = \sqrt{(2.45 \text{ m/s})^2 + (-2.98 \text{ m/s})^2}$

$v_{B2} = 3.86 \text{ m/s}$

$\tan \theta = \dfrac{v_{B2y}}{v_{B2x}} = \dfrac{2.98 \text{ m/s}}{2.45 \text{ m/s}} = 1.22$

$\theta = \tan^{-1}(1.22) = 50.6°$

$v_{B2} = 3.86 \text{ m/s}$ **to the right, 50.6° below the horizontal**

ANSWER KEY

Chapter 10

1. A store manager places ten paint cans into a rectangle five cans long and two cans wide on the floor. He then tells an assistant to stack the remaining cans on the floor into a pyramidal display so that the second level is similar to the first. The third and fourth levels are each made up of eight cans arranged in a 4 × 2-can rectangle. The rest of the display should have every other remaining level decreasing by 2 cans. How much work does the assistant do in lifting the cans into position if each can weighs 46.0 N and is 0.20 m tall?

   $W = Fd = F_g d$

Display row	Height (m)	Number of cans
2	0.20	10
3	0.40	8
4	0.60	8
5	0.80	6
6	1.00	6
7	1.20	4
8	1.40	4
9	1.60	2
10	1.80	2

   $W = (F)(d)$
   $= 46.0N[10(0.20\ m) + 8(0.40\ m)$
   $+ 8(0.60\ m) + 6(0.80\ m) + 6(1.00\ m)$
   $+ 4(1.20\ m) + 4(1.40\ m) + 2(1.60\ m)$
   $+ 2(1.80\ m)]$
   $= (46.0\ N)(38.0\ m)$

   $W = 1750\ N$

2. You exert a horizontal force of 4.6 N on a textbook sliding it 0.60 m across a library table to a friend.

   a. What amount of work do you do?

   $W = Fd = (4.6\ N)(0.60\ m)$
   $W = 2.8\ J$

   b. You friend in Problem 2 returns the book by pushing it with a force of 6.2 N at an angle of 30.0 below the horizontal. What amount of work does your friend do?

   $W = Fd \cos \theta$
   $= (6.2\ N)(0.60\ m) \cos(30.0°)$
   $W = 3.2\ J$

3. A ski lift whisks a 75-kg skier at 3.0 m/s for 1.5 minutes along a cable that is inclined at an angle of 40.0° from the horizontal.

   a. How much work was done by the ski lift?

   $F_y = mg$
   $d_y = vt \sin \theta$
   $W = mgvt \sin \theta = (75\ kg)(9.80\ m/s^2)$
   $(3.0\ m/s)(9.0 \times 10^1\ s) \sin(40.0°)$
   $W = 1.3 \times 10^5\ J$

   b. How much power is expended by the ski lift?

   $P = \dfrac{W}{t} = \dfrac{1.3 \times 10^5\ J}{9.0 \times 10^1\ s}$
   $P = 1.4 \times 10^3\ W = 1.4\ kW$

4. An engine that has a power output 1.2 MW is used to propel an airplane that weighs 1.5×10^5 N. What is the maximum vertical speed that the plane can attain?

   $P = \dfrac{W}{t} = \dfrac{Fd}{t} = F\dfrac{d}{t} = Fv$
   $P = F_g v_y;$
   $v_y = \dfrac{P}{F_g} = \dfrac{1.2 \times 10^6\ W}{1.5 \times 10^5\ N}$
   $v_y = 8.0\ m/s$

5. Armando expends 12 watts of power to maintain a horizontal swimming speed of 0.75 m/s.

   a. How much drag (resistance force) does the water exert on Armando?

   $P = \dfrac{W}{t} = \dfrac{Fd}{t} = F\dfrac{d}{t} = Fv$
   $F = \dfrac{P}{v} = \dfrac{12\ W}{0.75\ m/s} = 16\ N$

b. The drag on the swimmer is proportional to the square of the swimmer's speed. What power would Armando expend maintaining a swimming speed of 1.50 m/s?

$P = Fv$

$F \propto v^2$

$P \propto v^3$

$\dfrac{P_1}{P_2} = \dfrac{v_1^3}{v_2^3}; P_2 = P_1\left(\dfrac{v_2}{v_1}\right)^3$

$P_2 = 12 \text{ W}\left(\dfrac{1.5 \text{ m/s}}{0.75 \text{ m/s}}\right)^3$

$P_2 = 96 \text{ W}$

6. A 40.0-N sack is attached to the wheel of a wheel-and-axle, which has a wheel-diameter of 30.00 cm and an axle-diameter of 6.00 cm.

a. What is the IMA of the wheel-and-axle?

$IMA = \dfrac{r_e}{r_r} = \dfrac{(30.00 \text{ cm}/2)}{(6.00 \text{ cm}/2)}$

$IMA = 5.00$

b. If the effort force moves 0.40 m, what distance is the machine designed to lift the sack?

$IMA = \dfrac{d_e}{d_r}; d_r = \dfrac{d_e}{IMA}$

$d_r = \dfrac{0.40 \text{ m}}{5.00} = 0.080 \text{ m}$

7. A 40.0-N sack is attached to the axle of the wheel-and-axle in Problem 6. Calculate the IMA and the distance the sack moves if the effort moves 0.40 m.

$IMA = \dfrac{r_e}{r_r} = \dfrac{(6.00 \text{ cm}/2)}{(30.00 \text{ cm}/2)}$

$IMA = 0.200 \text{ m}$

$d_r = \dfrac{d_e}{IMA} = \dfrac{0.40 \text{ m}}{0.200} = 2.0 \text{ m}$

8. Leah is helping to build a water habitat in a neighborhood park. The habitat includes an upper pond connected to a lower pond, 3.2 m below, by a trickling stream with several small cascades. At a home-building store, she finds a 45-W pump that has a maximum circulation rate of 1900 liters of water per hour. Determine if the pump is powerful enough to raise the water from the lower to upper pond? (The mass density of water, ρ, is 1.00 kg/L)

$P = \dfrac{Fd}{t} = \dfrac{mgd}{t}$

$m = \rho V$

$P = \dfrac{\rho V g d}{t}$

$= \dfrac{(1.00 \text{ kg/L})(1900 \text{ L})(9.80 \text{ m/s}^2)(3.2 \text{ m})}{3600 \text{ s}}$

$P = 17 \text{ W}$

The 45-W pump will work.

9. Using a block-and-tackle, a mover takes up 18.5 m of rope to raise a 115-kg stove from the ground to a window ledge 3.7 m high. What force must he exert on the rope if the efficiency of the block-and-tackle is 63%?

$\text{efficiency (\%)} = \dfrac{W_o}{W_i} \times 100 = \dfrac{F_r d_r}{F_e d_e} \times 100$

$F_e = \dfrac{F_r d_r}{\text{efficiency } d_e} \times 100$

$F_e = \dfrac{mg d_r}{\text{efficiency } d_e} \times 100$

$= \dfrac{(115 \text{ kg})(9.80 \text{ m/s}^2)(3.7 \text{ m})}{(63\%)(18.5 \text{ m})} \times 100$

$F_e = 360 \text{ N}$

Physics: Principles and Problems

10. While unpacking a blind to hang, Rahul sees that the shaft of the blind, which rotates the horizontal slats, is connected to a small gearbox. The gearbox is also connected to the wand, which is turned to open and close the slats as shown below.

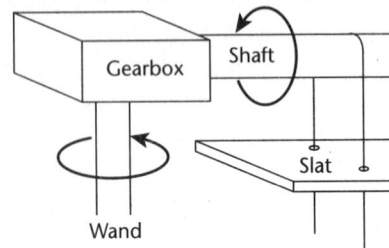

Rahul measures the wand's diameter as 1.00 cm and the shaft's diameter as 1.25 cm. He notes that to rotate the slats 180°, the wand has to make three complete rotations. Rahul concludes that the gearbox contains what ratio of the gear teeth?

$$IMA = \frac{d_e}{d_r} = \frac{\text{teeth on shaft sprocket}}{\text{teeth on wand sprocket}}$$
$$\times \frac{\text{wand radius}}{\text{shaft radius}}$$

$d_e = 3(2\pi)(\text{wand radius}) = 6\pi(\text{wand radius})$
$d_r = 1/2(2\pi)(\text{shaft radius}) = \pi (\text{shaft radius})$

$$\frac{6\pi \text{ wand radius}}{\pi \text{ shaft radius}} = \frac{\text{teeth on shaft sprocket}}{\text{teeth on wand sprocket}}$$
$$\times \frac{\text{wand radius}}{\text{shaft radius}}$$

$$\frac{6}{1} = \frac{\text{teeth on shaft sprocket}}{\text{teeth on wand sprocket}}$$

Chapter 11

1. Rae Ann weighs 530 N. What is her kinetic energy as she swims at a speed of 1.2 m/s?

   $K = 1/2\ mv^2$
   $F_g = mg$
   $K = \frac{1}{2}\frac{F_g v^2}{g} = \frac{1}{2}\frac{(530\ N)(1.2\ m/s)^2}{9.80\ m/s^2}$
   $K = 39$ J

2. In a hardware store, paint cans, which weigh 46 N each, are transported from storage to the back of the paint department by placing them on a 24°-ramp. The cans slide down the ramp at a constant speed of 3.4 m/s onto a table made of the same material as the ramp. How far does each can slide on the table?

   On the ramp
   $F_f = \mu F_N$
   $F_f = F_p = F_g \sin \theta$
   $F_N = F_g \cos \theta$
   $F_g \sin \theta = \mu F_g \cos \theta$
   $\mu = \frac{\sin \theta}{\cos \theta} = \tan \theta = \tan (24°)$

   On the table
   $W = \Delta K$
   $F_f d = 1/2(mv^2 - mv_0^2)$
   $d = \frac{0 - mv_0^2}{2F_f}$
   $F_f = \mu F_N = -\mu F_g$
   $d = \frac{-(F_g/g)v_0^2}{-2 \tan \theta F_g} = \frac{v_0^2}{2g \tan \theta}$
   $= \frac{(3.4\ m/s)^2}{2(9.80\ m/s^2)\tan (24°)}$
   $d = 1.3$ m

3. Zeke begins to slide down a snow hill on a rubber mat. Zeke's mass is 76 kg and that of the mat is 2 kg.

   a. What is the change in the gravitational potential energy of Zeke and the mat when they are 1.2 m below the crest?

   $\Delta U_g = U_{g2} - U_{g1}$
   $= mgh_2 - mgh_1 = mg\Delta h$
   $= (78\ kg)(9.80\ m/s^2)(-1.2\ m)$
   $\Delta U_g = -920$ J

   b. Disregarding frictional forces, what is the change in the kinetic energy of Zeke and the mat when they are 1.2 m below the crest?

   $K_1 + U_{g1} = K_2 + U_{g2}$
   $\Delta K = K_2 - K_1 = U_{g1} - U_{g2}$
   $= -(U_{g2} - U_{g1}) = -\Delta U_g$
   $\Delta K = +920$ J

c. Disregarding frictional forces, how fast are they moving when they are 1.2 m below the crest?

$\Delta K = K_2 - K_1; \quad K_1 = 0$

$K_2 = \Delta K$

$1/2 mv_2^2 = \Delta K$

$v_2 = \sqrt{\dfrac{2\Delta K}{m}} = \sqrt{\dfrac{2(920 \text{ J})}{78 \text{ kg}}}$

$v_2 = 4.9$ m/s

4. Kim is playing with a bead that slides on a wire as shown below.

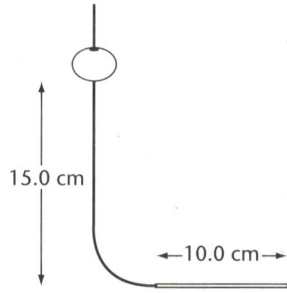

15.0 cm

←10.0 cm→

The wire and bead are frictionless but the white sheathing exerts a constant frictional force on the 5.0-g bead.

a. When the bead is dropped as shown, it comes to rest 6.0 cm along the white sheathing. How much work does the white sheathing do on the bead?

Along the wire

$U_{g1} + K_1 = U_{g2} + K_2$

$h_2 = 0; U_{g2} = 0$

$v_1 = 0; K_1 = 0$

$U_{g1} = K_2$

Along the white sheathing

$W = \Delta K = K_3 - K_2$

$v_3 = 0, K_3 = 0$

$W = -K_2$

$W = -U_{g1} = -mgh$

$= -(5.0 \times 10^{-3} \text{ kg})(9.80 \text{ m/s}^2)$
$(1.5 \times 10^{-1} \text{ m})$

$W = -7.4 \times 10^{-3}$ J

b. From what height should the bead be dropped so it stops at the end of the white sheathing?

From 4a,

$W = -F_f d$

$F_f = \dfrac{W}{d} = -7.4 \times 10^{-3}$ J/6.0×10^{-2} m

$F_f = 1.2 \times 10^{-1}$ N

$W = -U_{g1}$

$-F_f d = -mgh$

$h = \dfrac{-F_f d}{-mg}$

$= \dfrac{(1.2 \times 10^{-1} \text{ N})(1.00 \times 10^{-1} \text{ m})}{(5.0 \times 10^{-3} \text{ kg})(9.80 \text{ m/s}^2)}$

$h = 0.24$ m

6. Running at 4.0 m/s, Rafael grabs a vertical rope and swings upward. Assuming that air resistance is negligible, how far does Rafael rise?

$U_{g1} + K_1 = U_{g2} + K_2$

$U_{g1} = 0, K_2 = 0$

$U_{g2} = K_1$

$mgh = 1/2\ mv^2$

$h = \dfrac{v^2}{2g} = \dfrac{(4.0 \text{ m/s})^2}{2(9.80 \text{ m/s}^2)}$

$h = 0.82$ m

Physics: Principles and Problems

ANSWER KEY

7. A coiled spring gives a block of wood a kinetic energy of 1.50 J. The block slides up a ramp to a height that is 0.880 the height predicted using the conservation of mechanical energy.

   a. Plot graphs showing the gravitational potential energy and kinetic energy of the brick at the bottom of the incline and at the point where it comes to rest.

   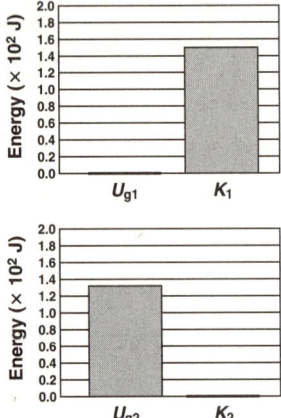

   $K_1 = 1.50$ J

   $U_{g1} = 0$

   $K_2 = 0$

   $U_{g2} = mgh_2 = mg(0.880)h_3$
   $= 0.880 mgh_3$

   From the conservation of mechanical energy

   $U_{g3} = K_1$

   $U_{g2} = 0.880 U_{g3} = 0.880 K_1$
   $= (0.880)(1.50 \text{ J})$

   $U_{g2} = 1.32$ J

   b. How much mechanical energy was lost?

   $E_{lost} = 0.880 K_1 - K_1 = -0.120 K_1$
   $= -0.120(1.50 \text{ J})$

   $E_{lost} = -0.180$ J

8. Erin raises the 1.20-kg bob of a pendulum to a level at which its gravitational potential energy is 3.00 J.

   a. Predict the speed of the bob as it passes through its lowest point.

   $E = U_{g1} + K_1 + U_{g2} + K_2$

   $U_{g2} = 0, K_1 = 0$

   $E = K_2$

   $1/2 mv_2^2 = E$

   $v_2 = \sqrt{\dfrac{2E}{m}} = \sqrt{\dfrac{2(3.00 \text{ J})}{1.20 \text{ kg}}}$

   $v_2 = 2.24$ m/s

   b. Erin releases the bob from rest and uses a photogate to measure its speed as it passes through its lowest point. She finds that the speed is 93.2% of the predicted value. How much work did frictional forces do on the pendulum?

   $v' = 0.932 v_2 = (0.932)(2.24 \text{ m/s})$
   $= 2.09$ m/s

   $K' = 1/2 mv'^2 = 1/2(1.20 \text{ kg})(2.09 \text{ m/s})^2$

   $K' = 2.62$ J

   $W = \Delta K = K' - K_1 = 2.62 \text{ J} - 3.00 \text{ J}$

   $W = -0.38$ J

   c. The pendulum's original energy was decreased by what percentage due to the work done by frictional forces on the pendulum as it moved from its release point through its lowest point?

   % energy decrease $= \dfrac{W}{E} \times 100$

   $= \dfrac{-0.38 \text{ J}}{3.0 \text{ J}} \times 100$

   % energy decrease $= 13$%

9. Steve can consistently throw a 0.200-kg ball at a speed of 12.0 m/s. On one throw the ball passes the top of a flagpole, which is 6.00 m above the ball's initial position.

   a. What is the ball's gravitational potential energy when it passes the top of the flagpole? (Assume the ball's initial gravitational energy is 0 J).

   $U_{g2} = mgh_2$
   $= (0.200 \text{ kg})(9.80 \text{ m/s}^2)(6.00 \text{ m})$

   $U_{g2} = 11.8$ J

   b. What is the ball's kinetic energy as it passes the top of the flagpole?

   $K_2 = K_1 - U_{g2} = 1/2 mv_2^2 - U_{g2}$

94 Supplemental Problems Answer Key

ANSWER KEY

$K_2 = 1/2(0.200 \text{ kg})(12.0 \text{ m/s})^2 - 11.8 \text{ J}$

$K_2 = 14.4 \text{ J} - 11.8 \text{ J} = 2.6 \text{ J}$

c. Steve throws the ball straight upward. What is the ball's velocity as it first passes the top of the flagpole?

$K_2 = 1/2 mv_2^2$

$v_2 = \sqrt{\dfrac{2K_2}{m}} = \sqrt{\dfrac{2(2.6 \text{ J})}{0.20 \text{ kg}}}$

$v_2 = 5.1$ m/s, upward

d. Steve throws the ball at a speed of 12.0 m/s so that it just reaches the top of the flagpole. What is the ball's velocity at the top of the flagpole?

$K_2 = 1/2 mv_2^2$

$v_2 = \sqrt{\dfrac{2K_2}{m}} = \sqrt{\dfrac{2(2.6 \text{ J})}{0.20 \text{ kg}}}$

$v_2 = 5.1$ m/s, horizontally

e. For question 9 d, what is the ball's initial velocity?

$\cos\theta = \dfrac{v_2}{v} = \dfrac{5.1 \text{ m/s}}{12.0 \text{ m/s}} = 0.43$

$\theta = \cos^{-1}(0.43) = 65°$

$v = 12.0$ m/s, 65° above the horizontal

10. A skateboarding area has two ramps. The first ramp has a height of 0.30 m and the second a height of 0.60 m. A 2.0-kg skateboard is released from rest at the top of the first ramp and rolls down the ramp onto the level ground. There a 47-kg skateboarder jumps on it and rides it up the second ramp. With what horizontal velocity must the skateboarder mount the skateboard as it moves on the level so that the board just reaches the top of the second ramp? (Assume that frictional forces on the skateboard wheels are negligible.)

On the first ramp

$U_{g1} + K_1 = U_{g2} + K_2$

$K_1 = 0, U_{g2} = 0$

$K_2 = U_{g1} = m_{\text{skateboard}} gh_1$

On the second ramp

$K_1 = U_{g2} = (m_{\text{skateboard}} + m_{\text{skateboarder}})gh_2$

On the level

$K_{\text{skateboard}} + K_{\text{skateboarder}} = K_{\text{skateboard + skateboarder}}$

$K_{\text{skateboarder}} = K_{\text{skateboard + skateboarder}} - K_{\text{skateboard}}$

$K_{\text{skateboarder}} = (m_{\text{skateboard}} + m_{\text{skateboarder}})gh_2 - m_{\text{skateboard}}gh_1$

$K_{\text{skateboarder}} = (m_{\text{skateboard}})g(h_2 - h_1) + (m_{\text{skateboarder}})gh_2$

$1/2 mv^2_{\text{skateboard}} = (m_{\text{skateboard}})g(h_2 - h_1) + m_{\text{skateboarder}}gh_2$

$v = \sqrt{2g\left(\dfrac{(m_{\text{skateboard}})(h_2 - h_1)}{m_{\text{skateboarder}}} + h_2\right)}$

$v = 3.5$ m/s in the direction of motion

Chapter 12

1. The freezing point of bromine –7.25°C. Its boiling point is 59.35°C.

   What is the state of bromine at the following temperatures?

   a. 251 K

   $T_K = T_C + 273$

   $T_C = T_K - 273 = 251 \text{ K} - 273 \text{ K}$

   $T_C = -22°\text{C}$; solid

   b. 305 K

   $T_C = T_K - 273 = 305 \text{ K} - 273 \text{ K}$

   $T_C = 32°\text{C}$; liquid

   c. 342 K

   $T_C = T_K - 273 = 342 \text{ K} - 273 \text{ K}$

   $T_C = 69°\text{C}$; gas

2. Octane, a substance found in petroleum, boils at 126°C and is a liquid over a range of 183 Celsius degrees. What is the melting point of octane in kelvins?

   Liquid range

   $126°\text{C} - 183°\text{C} = -57°\text{C}$

   Melting point is $-57°\text{C}$

   $T_K = T_C + 273 = -57°\text{C} + 273°\text{C}$

   $T_K = 216$ K

Physics: Principles and Problems   *Supplemental Problems Answer Key*   **95**

ANSWER KEY

3. How much energy is required to heat a clay pizza baking stone, which has a specific heat of 860 J/kg·K, from 25°C to 235°C? The mass of the stone is 4.8 kg.

   $Q = mC\Delta T = mC(T_f - T_i) = (4.8 \text{ kg})(860 \text{ J/kg·°C})(235°C - 25°C)$

   $Q = 8.7 \times 10^5 \text{ J}$

4. A 2.0-kg slab of concrete requires 11 kJ to raise its temperature from 23°C to 29°C. What is the specific heat of concrete?

   $Q = mC\Delta T = mC(T_f - T_i)$

   $C = \dfrac{Q}{m(T_f - T_i)} = \dfrac{11 \times 10^3 \text{ J}}{(2.0 \text{ kg})(29.0°C - 23.0°C)}$

   $C = 9.2 \times 10^2 \text{ J/kg·°C}$

5. A blacksmith lifts a 0.73-kg iron horseshoe from a forge at a temperature of 835°C and quenches the shoe in 45 kg of water at 23°C. What is the final temperature of the horseshoe and water?

   Iron $m_A = 0.73$ kg:

   $C_A = 450$ J/kg·°C

   $T_{Ai} = 835°C$

   Water $m_B = 45$ kg:

   $C_B = 4180$ J/kg·°C

   $T_{Bi} = 23°C$

   $T_f = \dfrac{m_A C_A T_{Ai} + m_B C_B T_{Bi}}{m_A C_A + m_B C_B}$

   $T_f = \dfrac{(0.73 \text{ kg})(450 \text{ J/kg·°C})(835°C) + (45 \text{ kg})(4180 \text{ J/kg·°C})(23°C)}{(0.73 \text{ kg})(450 \text{ J/kg·°C}) + (45 \text{ kg})(4180 \text{ J/kg·°C})}$

   $T_f = 24°C$

6. A silversmith pours 55.0 g of molten silver at 975°C into a mold and lets it cool to 25°C. How much heat does the silver transfer to the environment? The melting point of silver is 961°C and the specific heat of molten silver is 288J/kg·K.

   Cooling liquid silver

   $Q_1 = mC\Delta T = mC(T_f - T_i)$

   $= (.0550 \text{ kg})(288 \text{ J/kg·°C})(961°C - 975°C)$

   $Q_1 = -220 \text{ J}$

   Solidifying silver (from Table 12-2)

   $Q_2 = -mH_f = (0.0550 \text{ g})(1.04 \times 10^5 \text{ J/kg})$

   $Q_2 = -5720 \text{ J}$

   Cooling solid silver (from Table 12-1)

   $Q_3 = mC\Delta T = mC(T_f - T_i) = (0.0550 \text{ kg})(235 \text{ J/kg·°C})(25°C - 961°C)$

   $Q_3 = -12100 \text{ J}$

   $Q = Q_1 + Q_2 + Q_3 = (-220 \text{ J}) + (-5720 \text{ J}) + (-12100 \text{ J})$

   $Q = -1.80 \times 10^4 \text{ J}$

ANSWER KEY

7. Angie adds a block of ice at −4°C to cool 2.2 kg of water at 42°C in an insulated jug. When the water has cooled to 5°C, she removes the remaining ice. What is the mass of water in the jug?

   Cooling original mass of water

   $Q = mC_A \Delta T = (2.2 \text{ kg})(4180)(5°C - 42°C)$

   $Q = -3.4 \times 10^5 \text{ J}$

   Melting ice and raising its temperature

   $Q = mC_1 \Delta T_1 + mH_f + mC_2 \Delta T_2$

   $Q = -(-3.4 \times 10^5 \text{ J})$

   $m = \dfrac{Q}{C_B \Delta T_1 + H_f + C_A \Delta T_2}$

   $= \dfrac{3.4 \times 10^5 \text{ J}}{(2080 \text{ J/kg·°C})(0°C - (-4°C)) + (3.34 \times 10^5 \text{ J/kg}) + (4180 \text{ J/kg·°C})(5°C - 0°C)}$

   $m = 0.94 \text{ kg}$

   $m_T = m_1 + m_2 = 2.2 \text{ kg} + 0.94 \text{ kg}$

   $m_T = 3.1 \text{ kg}$

8. A cubic meter of water in a perfectly insulated container is exposed to solar energy during a 24-hour period as shown below.

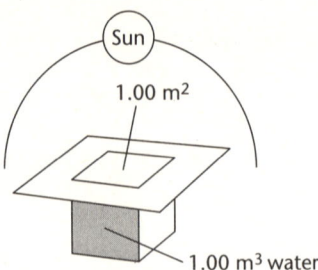

At the end of the 24 hours, the temperature of the water increases by 0.60°C. If all the solar energy was absorbed by the water though a 1.00 m² surface, what is the daily solar energy intensity measured in J/m²? (The density of water is 1.00×10^3 kg/m³.)

$Q = E$

$Q = mC\Delta T$

$E = mC\Delta T = \rho V C \Delta T$

$= (1.00 \times 10^3 \text{ kg/m}^3)(1.00 \text{ m}^3)$
$(4.180 \times 10^3 \text{ J/kg} \cdot °C)(0.60°C)$
$= 2.5 \times 10^6 \text{ J}$

$I = \dfrac{E}{A} = \dfrac{2.5 \times 10^6 \text{ J}}{1.00 \text{ m}^2}$

$I = 2.5 \times 10^6 \text{ J/m}^2$

Chapter 13

1. Marcos sets a can of paint, which weighs 46 N, on a shelf. The bottom of the paint can has a small lip on the which the can sits. The outer diameter of the lip is 16.8 cm and has a width of 2 mm. What pressure does the lip exert on the shelf?

$P = \dfrac{F}{A} = \dfrac{F}{\pi R_1^2 - \pi R_2^2}$

$= \dfrac{46 \text{ N}}{\pi((0.084 \text{ m})^2 - (0.082 \text{ m})^2)}$

$P = 44 \text{ kPa}$

2. During a 12-h period, the atmospheric pressure varied from 98 kPa to 105 kPa. By how much did the force acting on a 1.0-cm² patch of your skin vary?

$P = \dfrac{F}{A}$

$F = PA$

$\Delta F = \Delta PA = (105 \text{ kPa} - 98 \text{ kPa})(1.0 \text{ cm}^2)$
$= (7 \times 10^3 \text{ Pa})(1.0 \text{ cm}^2)(10^{-2} \text{ m/cm})^2$

$\Delta F = 0.7 \text{ N}$

3. With its full compliment of passengers, crew, and cargo, the *RMS Titanic* is reported to have a displacement of about 4.7×10^3 m³ of water. What was the ship's weight?

$F_{apparent} = F_g - F_{buoyant} = 0$

$F_g = F_{buoyant} = \rho_{water} g V$
$= (1.0 \times 10^3 \text{ kg/m}^3)(9.80 \text{ m/s}^2)$
$(4.7 \times 10^3 \text{ m}^3)$

$F_g = 4.6 \times 10^7 \text{ N}$

4. A spherical balloon, filled with helium, is tethered to the ground by a string. If the tension in the string is 7.5 N, what is the volume of the balloon? (Ignore the mass of the balloon.) The mass densities of air and helium are 1.2 kg/m³ and 0.177 kg/m³, respectively.

$F_{apparent} = F_g - F_{buoyant}$

$F_{apparent} = \rho_{air} g V - \rho_{He} g V = g V(\rho_{air} - \rho_{He})$

$V = \dfrac{F_{apparent}}{g(\rho_{air} - \rho_{He})}$

$= \dfrac{7.5 \text{ N}}{(9.80 \text{ m/s}^2)(1.2 \text{ kg/m}^3 - 0.177 \text{ kg/m}^3)}$

$V = 0.75 \text{ m}^3$

5. Exploring an ancient shipwreck off the coast of Greece, an underwater archeologist is in a submersible that reaches a depth of 3.00 km.

   a. What is the external pressure on the submersible if the density of seawater is 1.04×10^3 kg/m³ at this depth?

   $P = \rho_{seawater} g h$
   $= (1.04 \times 10^3 \text{ kg/m}^3)(9.80 \text{ m/s}^2)$
   $(3.00 \times 10^3 \text{ m})$

   $P = 3.06 \times 10^7 \text{ Pa}$

b. If the interior of the submersible is maintained at a pressure of 101 kPa, what force acts on a porthole that has a diameter of 10.0 cm?

$$P = \frac{F}{A}$$

$F = PA = (P_{exterior} - P_{interior})A$
$= (3.06 \times 10^7 \text{ Pa} - 0.0101 \times 10^7 \text{ Pa})$
  $\times (\pi(0.100 \text{ m})^2/4)$

$F = 2.40 \times 10^5 \text{ N}$

6. What does a coffee mug, which has a volume of 8×10^{-5} m³ and weighs 3.3 N in air, weigh submerged in a sink full of water?

$F_{apparent} = F_g - F_{buoyant}$
$= F_g - \rho_{water}gV$
$= 3.3 \text{ N} - (1.0 \times 10^3 \text{ kg/m})$
  $(9.80 \text{ m/s}^2)(8 \times 10^{-5} \text{ m}^3)$
$= 3.3 \text{ N} - 0.8 \text{ N}$

$F_{apparent} = 2.5 \text{ N}$

7. On a lakeshore, Leon finds a log that has a diameter of 0.16 m and a length of 2.0 m. He rolls the log, weighing 280 N, into the lake. What is the maximum weight the floating log can carry without submerging?

$V = \left(\pi \left(\frac{0.16 \text{ m}}{2}\right)^2\right) 2.0 \text{ m} = 0.040 \text{ m}^3$

$F_{apparent} = F_g - F_{buoyant} = 0$
$F_g = F_{buoyant} = \rho_{water}gV$
$= (1.0 \times 10^3 \text{ kg/m}^3)(9.80 \text{ m/s}^2)(0.040 \text{ m}^3)$
$F_g = 390 \text{ N}$
$F_g = F_{g1} + F_{g2}$
$F_{g2} = F_g - F_{g1} = 390 \text{ N} - 280 \text{ N}$
$F_{g2} = 110 \text{ N}$

The maximum weight is slightly less than 110 N.

8. In a foundry a worker heats a 27-cm long iron spike from 20°C to a temperature of 950°C in a forge. By how much has the length of the spike increased?

$\Delta L = \alpha L \Delta T = \alpha L(T_f - T_i)$
$= (1.2 \times 10^{-5} \text{°C}^{-1})(0.27 \text{ m})(950\text{°C} - 20\text{°C})$
$\Delta L = 3.0 \times 10^{-3} \text{ m}$

9. A helium-filled balloon, which has an initial volume of 8.0 m³ at 28°C, is placed in a hangar at an airport. Overnight the interior temperature of the hangar falls from 28°C to 13°C. What is the volume of the balloon the next morning?

$V_2 = V_1 + \beta V_1 \Delta T = V_1(1 + \beta(T_f - T_i))$
$= 8.0 \text{ m}^3(1 + (3.4 \times 10^{-3}\text{°C}^{-1})$
  $(13\text{°C} - 28\text{°C}))$
$= 8.0 \text{ m}^3(1 - 0.051)$
$= 7.6 \text{ m}^3$

10. What buoyancy was lost overnight by the helium-filled balloon in Problem 9? Assume the density of air is 1.2 kg/m³.

$\Delta F_{buoyancy} = \rho_{air}g\Delta V = \rho_{air}g(V_f - V_i)$
$= (1.2 \text{ kg/m}^3)(9.80 \text{ m/s}^2)(-0.4 \text{ m}^3)$
$\Delta F_{buoyancy} = -5 \text{ N}$

Chapter 14

1. Sonya hears water dripping from the eaves of the house onto a porch roof. She counts 20 drops in one minute.

a. What is the period of the drops?

$T = 60 \text{ s}/20 \text{ drops} = 3 \text{ s}$

b. What is the frequency of the drops?

$f = \frac{1}{T} = \frac{1}{3 \text{ s}}$

$f = 0.3 \text{ Hz}$

2. You scrape a long nail across a metal file. The speed of the nail is 25 cm/s and the file has groves that are 1.0 mm apart. What is the frequency of the "clicks" made by the nail?

$\bar{v} = \frac{d}{t}$

$t = \frac{d}{\bar{v}} = \frac{1.0 \times 10^{-1} \text{ cm}}{25 \text{ cm/s}}$

$t = 0.0040 \text{ s}$

$f = \frac{1}{T} = \frac{1}{0.0040 \text{ s}}$

$f = 250 \text{ Hz}$

Physics: Principles and Problems *Supplemental Problems Answer Key*

3. Hiroshi is generating waves on a rope by flipping the rope up and down. Each motion up or down lasts 0.20 s. The distance from a crest to a trough is 0.40 m.

   a. What is the amplitude of the wave?

   $A = 1/2$ **distance from crest to trough**
   $= 1/2 \ (0.40 \text{ m})$

   $A = 0.20 \text{ m}$

   b. What is the frequency of the waves?

   $T = t_{up} + t_{down} = (0.20 \text{ s} + 0.20 \text{ s})$
   $= 0.40 \text{ s}$

   $f = \dfrac{1}{T} = \dfrac{1}{0.40 \text{ s}}$

   $f = 2.5 \text{ Hz}$

4. Ripples in a pond each have a wavelength of 8.0 cm and frequency of 3.0 Hz. What is the speed of a ripple?

   $v = \lambda f = (8.0 \text{ cm})(3.0 \text{ Hz})$

   $v = 24 \text{ cm/s}$

5. A Love wave, one of the four types of waves associated with earthquakes, is a transverse wave in which the surface of the earth moves back and forth as the wave passes. What is the period of a Love wave that has speed of 4.1 km/s and a wavelength of 620 km?

   $v = \lambda f$

   $f = \dfrac{1}{T}$

   $v = \dfrac{\lambda}{T}$

   $T = \dfrac{\lambda}{v} = \dfrac{620 \text{ km}}{4.1 \text{ km/s}}$

   $T = 150 \text{ s}$

6. Two pulses, one with a length of 0.30 m and an amplitude of 0.24 m and the other with a length of 0.54 m and an amplitude of −0.13 m, approach each other on a rope.

   a. What is the amplitude of the rope at the point where the midpoints of the pulses pass each other?

   $A = A_1 + A_2 = 0.24 \text{ m} + (-0.13 \text{ m})$

   $A = 0.11 \text{ m}$

   b. What is the pulse length when the midpoints of the pulses pass each other?

   0.54 m

7. Figure 14-1a shows a pulse traveling at a speed of 1.0 m/s in a coiled spring to which a second spring is attached at point A. Figure 14-1b shows the springs a few moments later.

   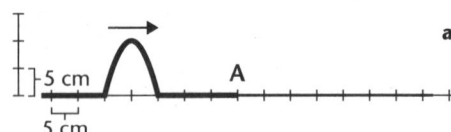
   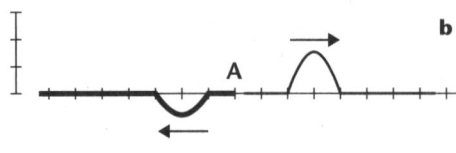

   Figure 14-1

   a. What is the amplitude of the incident pulse?

   10 cm

   b. What is the speed of the reflected pulse?

   1.0 m/s

   c. What is the speed of the transmitted pulse?

   $\overline{v}_{reflected} = \dfrac{d}{t}$

   $t = \dfrac{d}{\overline{v}_{reflected}} = \dfrac{0.10 \text{ m}}{1.0 \text{ m/s}}$

   $t = 0.10 \text{ s}$

   $\overline{v}_{transmitted} = \dfrac{d}{t} = \dfrac{0.15 \text{ m}}{0.10 \text{ s}}$

   $\overline{v}_{transmitted} = 1.5 \text{ m/s}$

8. In Figure 14-2 a pulse is traveling at a speed of 1.0 m/s in a coiled spring to which a second spring is attached at point A. Figure 14-2b shows the location of the transmitted pulse, which has a speed of 0.80 m/s.

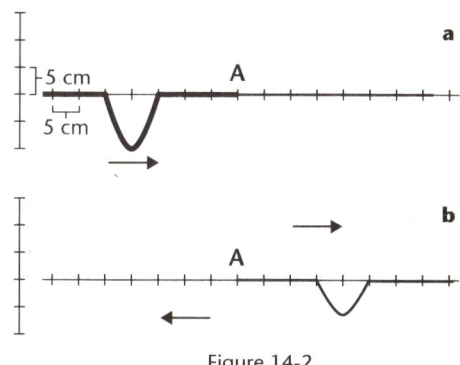

Figure 14-2

a. What is the speed of the reflected pulse?

   1.0 m/s

b. Is the reflected pulse erect or inverted?

   The reflected pulse is erect.

9. A physics teacher attaches an electric oscillator to one end of a 2.0-m long, horizontal spring and attaches the other end to a stationary hook in a wall. She adjusts the frequency of the oscillator to produce a standing wave in the spring. Students observe that the standing wave has 3 nodes and 2 antinodes. She then doubles the frequency of the oscillations and produces another standing wave. How many nodes and antinodes do the students observe in the standing wave?

   For f_1, 3 nodes and 2 antinodes indicate that the standing wave has a wavelength of 2.0 m.

   $\lambda_1 = 2.0$ m

   $f_2 = 2f_1$

   $v = \lambda_1 f_1 = \lambda_2 f_2$

   $(2.0 \text{ m})f_1 = \lambda_2(2f_1)$

   $\lambda_2 = 1.0$ m

   The standing wave contains two 2 full wavelengths; therefore, the students observe 5 nodes and 4 antinodes.

10. A water wave with a wavelength of 7.0 cm and speed of 21 cm/s moves into a more shallow part of a pond where its wavelength is 6.0 cm.

    a. What is the frequency of the wave on the shallow water?

    $v = \lambda f$

    $f = \dfrac{v}{\lambda} = \dfrac{21 \text{ cm/s}}{7.0 \text{ cm}} = 3.0$ Hz

    b. What is the velocity of the wave in the more shallow water?

    $v = \lambda f = (3.0 \text{ Hz})(6.0 \text{ cm})$

    $v = 18$ cm/s

Chapter 15

Assume the speed of sound in air is 343 m/s unless otherwise noted.

1. Animal behavior researchers hypothesize that elephants communicate by producing and detecting low-pitched sounds. The sound waves of one such sound have a frequency of 150 Hz. What is the wavelength of the sound wave?

   $v = \lambda f$

   $\lambda = \dfrac{v}{f} = \dfrac{343 \text{ m/s}}{150 \text{ Hz}}$

   $\lambda = 2.3$ m

2. Wayne is swimming underwater in a lake when a large rock falls from a ledge into the lake. If Wayne is 75 m from the place where the rock enters the water, at what time later will Wayne hear the splash? The speed of sound is 1460 m/s in cool lake water.

   $v = \dfrac{d}{t}$

   $t = \dfrac{d}{v} = \dfrac{75 \text{ m}}{1460 \text{ m/s}}$

   $t = 0.051$ s

ANSWER KEY

For questions 3–5 use the following information.

The equation for the Doppler shift of a wave of speed v reaching a moving detector is

$$f_d = f_s \frac{(v + v_d)}{(v - v_s)}$$

where v_d is the speed of the detector, v_s is the speed of the source, f_s is the frequency of the source, and f_d is the frequency of the detector. If the detector moves toward the source, v_d is positive, if the source moves toward the detector, v_s is positive.

3. While fishing off a boat anchored offshore, you note that the distance between successive wave crests is about 12 m and their speed is about 7.5 m/s.

   a. What is the frequency of the waves?

   $v = \lambda f$

   $f = \frac{v}{\lambda} = \frac{7.5 \text{ m/s}}{12 \text{ m}}$

   $f = 0.63$ Hz

   b. If the boat hoists anchor and heads out to sea at a speed of 15 m/s, what will you observe as the wave frequency?

   $v_s = 0$

   $f_d = f_s \frac{(v + v_d)}{(v - v_s)} = \frac{(v + v_d)}{v}$

   $f_d = 0.63 \text{ Hz} \frac{(7.5 \text{ m/s} + 15.0 \text{ m/s})}{7.5 \text{ m/s}}$

   $f_d = 1.9$ Hz

4. On board a fishing boat heading out to sea at a speed of 15 m/s, another fishing boat behind you sounds a 510-Hz horn as it heads toward the shore at a speed 18 m/s. What is the frequency of the sound waves from the horn that reach you?

   $f_d = f_s \frac{(v + v_d)}{(v - v_s)}$

   $= 510 \text{ Hz} \frac{(343 \text{ m/s} - 15 \text{ m/s})}{(343 \text{ m/s} + 18 \text{ m/s})}$

   $f_d = 460$ Hz

5. A species of bat navigates by emitting short bursts of sound waves that have a frequency range that peaks at 58.0 kHz.

   a. If the bat is flying at 4.0 m/s toward a stationary object, what is the frequency of the sound waves reaching the object?

   The frequency of the sound waves reaching stationary object is f_{d1}.

   $f_{d1} = f_s \frac{(v)}{(v - v_s)}$

   $= 58.0 \text{ kHz} \frac{(343 \text{ m/s})}{(343 \text{ m/s} - 4.0 \text{ m/s})}$

   $f_{d1} = 59$ kHz

   b. What is the frequency of the reflected sound waves detected by the bat?

   The frequency of the reflected sound waves from the object is f_{d1} and the frequency of the sound waves detected by the bat is f_{d2}.

   $f_{d2} = f_{d1} \frac{(v + v_d)}{(v)}$

   $= 59 \text{ kHz} \frac{(343 \text{ m/s} + 4.0 \text{ m/s})}{(343 \text{ m/s})}$

   $f_{d2} = 6.0 \times 10^1$ kHz

   c. What is the difference between the frequency of the sound waves emitted by the bat and the frequency of the sound waves detected by the bat if the bat is flying at 4.0 m/s and the object is a moth approaching at 1.0 m/s?

   $f_{d1} = f_s \frac{(v + v_d)}{(v - v_s)}$

   $= 58.0 \text{ kHz} \frac{(343 \text{ m/s} + 1.0 \text{ m/s})}{(343 \text{ m/s} - 4.0 \text{ m/s})}$

   $f_{d1} = 59$ kHz

   $f_{d2} = f_{d1} \frac{(v + v_d)}{(v - v_s)}$

   $= 59 \text{ kHz} \frac{(343 \text{ m/s} + 1.0 \text{ m/s})}{(343 \text{ m/s} - 4.0 \text{ m/s})}$

   $f_{d2} = 6.0 \times 10^1$ kHz

   $\Delta f = f_{d2} - f_s = 6.0 \times 10^1 \text{ kHz} - 58.0 \text{ kHz}$

   $\Delta f = 2$ kHz

ANSWER KEY

6. A monitor detects the pressure amplitude of the sound wave from a thunderclap as 6×10^{-1} Pa and displays the sound level as 90 dB. A second more distant monitor displays the sound level of the thunderclap as 70 dB. What pressure amplitude did the second monitor detect?

   For each 20 dB decrease, the pressure amplitude decreases by a factor of 10^{-1}. Therefore the pressure amplitude of a 70 dB sound is 1/10 the pressure amplitude of a 90 dB sound.

   $A_2 = (0.1)(A_1) = (0.1)(6 \times 10^{-1}$ Pa$)$

   $A_2 = 6 \times 10^{-2}$ Pa

7. The strings of a standard guitar are tuned to the following frequencies: 165, 220, 294, 392, 494, and 659 Hz.

   a. Find the lengths of open-ended organ pipes that would produce the same frequencies.

   $f = \dfrac{v}{2L}$

   $L = \dfrac{v}{2f}$

   $L_1 = \dfrac{v}{2f_1} = \dfrac{343 \text{ m/s}}{2(165 \text{ Hz})} = 1.04$ m

   $L_2 = \dfrac{v}{2f_2} = \dfrac{343 \text{ m/s}}{2(220 \text{ Hz})} = 0.780$ m

   $L_3 = \dfrac{v}{2f_3} = \dfrac{343 \text{ m/s}}{2(294 \text{ Hz})} = 0.583$ m

   $L_4 = \dfrac{v}{2f_4} = \dfrac{343 \text{ m/s}}{2(392 \text{ Hz})} = 0.438$ m

   $L_5 = \dfrac{v}{2f_5} = \dfrac{343 \text{ m/s}}{2(494 \text{ Hz})} = 0.347$ m

   $L_6 = \dfrac{v}{2f_6} = \dfrac{343 \text{ m/s}}{2(659 \text{ Hz})} = 0.260$ m

   b. Sketch the pipes showing their lengths to scale.

   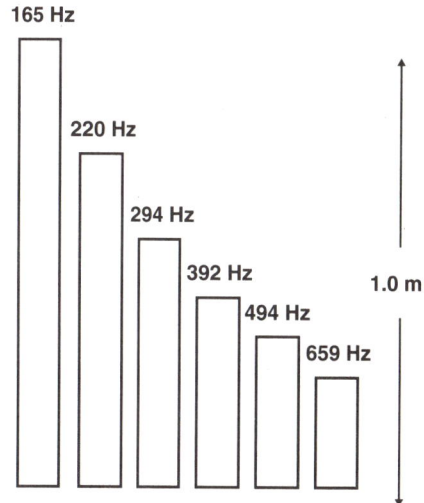

8. Carla takes a 22.0-cm length of rigid, plastic tubing and places it into a glass of water so that one end of the tube is submerged 3.0 cm. She gently blows across the opposite end of the tube. What frequency sound waves will the tube produce?

   $f = \dfrac{v}{4L} = \dfrac{343 \text{ m/s}}{4(0.220 \text{ m} - 0.030 \text{ m})}$

   $f = 451$ Hz

9. The fundamental tone of an open-pipe resonator with a length of 0.22 m is the same as the first harmonic of a closed-pipe resonator. What is the length of the closed-pipe resonator?

   $f_1 = \dfrac{v}{2L_1}$

   $3f_2 = f_1$

   $f_2 = \dfrac{v}{4L_2}$

   $\dfrac{3v}{4L_2} = \dfrac{v}{2L_1}$

   $L_2 = \dfrac{3}{2}L_1 = \dfrac{3}{2}(0.22 \text{ m})$

   $L_2 = 0.33$ m

Physics: Principles and Problems   Supplemental Problems Answer Key   103

ANSWER KEY

10. You receive a cassette tape with the following note. "The first sound on the tape is the sound of a 442-Hz tuning fork and a second tuning fork being struck simultaneously. The second sound on the tape is the sound of the second tuning fork and a 444-Hz tuning fork being struck simultaneously. What is the frequency of the second tuning fork?" Listening to the tape you hear that the first sound has a beat frequency of 3 Hz and the second sound has beat frequency of 5 Hz. Answer the question found in the note.

    $f_{beat} = |f_2 - f_1|$

    $(f_2 - f_1) = \pm f_{beat}$

    $f_2 = f_1 \pm f_{beat}$

    $f_2 = 442 \text{ Hz} \pm 3 \text{ Hz}$

    $f_2 = 445 \text{ hz or } 439 \text{ Hz}$

    $f_{beat} = |f_2 - f_3|$

    $(f_2 - f_3) = \pm f_{beat}$

    $f_2 = f_3 \pm f_{beat}$

    $f_2 = 444 \text{ Hz} \pm 5 \text{ Hz}$

    $f_2 = 449 \text{ Hz or } 439 \text{ Hz}$

    The frequency of the second tuning fork is 439 Hz.

Chapter 16

1. Calculate the frequency of violet light, $\lambda = 434$ nm.

    $c = \lambda f, f = \dfrac{c}{\lambda}$

    $f = \dfrac{3.00 \times 10^8 \text{ m/s}}{4.34 \times 10^{-11} \text{ m}} = 6.91 \times 10^{18} \text{ Hz}$

2. Calculate the wavelength of infrared radiation, $f = 2.66 \times 10^{13}$ Hz, as it travels through a vacuum.

    $c = \lambda f, \lambda = \dfrac{c}{f}$

    $\lambda = \dfrac{3.00 \times 10^8 \text{ m/s}}{2.66 \times 10^{13} \text{ m}} = 1.12 \times 10^{-5} \text{ m}$

3. When Mars and Earth are closest together in their orbits, they are about 5.4×10^7 km apart. When the two planets are most distant from each other, they are about 4.01×10^8 km apart. How much more time would it take for an astronomer on Earth to observe an event on Mars when the two planets are farthest apart compared to when the planets are closest together? Use the speed of light in a vacuum.

    $\Delta d = d_{farthest} - d_{closest}$

    $\Delta d = 4.01 \times 10^8 \text{ km} - 5.4 \times 10^7 \text{ km}$

    $= 3.47 \times 10^8 \text{ km}$

    Difference in time $= \Delta T = \dfrac{\Delta d}{c}$

    $\Delta t = \dfrac{3.47 \times 10^8 \text{ km}}{3.00 \times 10^8 \text{ m/s}} = \dfrac{3.47 \times 10^{11} \text{ m}}{3.00 \times 10^8 \text{ m/s}}$

    $= 1.16 \times 10^3 \text{ s}$

4. A 90-watt halogen "energy-saving" incandescent bulb has a light output of 1780 lm. What illumination will this bulb provide on a surface 39 cm from the bulb?

    Illuminance $= E = \dfrac{P}{4\pi d^2}$

    $E = \dfrac{1780 \text{ lm}}{4\pi (0.39 \text{ m})^2} = 930 \text{ lx}$

5. What is the luminous flux of an incandescent bulb that provides illumination of 84.5 lx at a distance of 1.32 m from the bulb?

    Luminous flux $= P$

    $E = \dfrac{P}{4\pi d^2}, P = 4\pi d^2 E$

    $P = 4\pi (1.32 \text{ m})^2 (84.5 \text{ lx}) = 1850 \text{ lm}$

6. Calculate the candle power of an incandescent bulb that provides 1580 lm of luminous flux.

    $P = 4\pi I, I = \dfrac{P}{4\pi}$

    $I = \dfrac{1580 \text{ lm}}{4\pi} = 126 \text{ cd}$

7. Calculate the candle power of a point source of light that provides 1330 lx of illumination at a distance of 8.00 m.

   Candle power = $I = \dfrac{P}{4\pi}$

   Luminous flux = $P = 4\pi d^2 E$

   so, $I = \dfrac{4\pi d^2 E}{4\pi} = d^2 E$

   $I = (8.00 \text{ m})^2(1330 \text{ lx}) = 85\ 100 \text{ cd}$

8. What illumination does the light source in problem 7 provide at a distance of 2.00 m?

   Applying the universe square law,

   $\dfrac{E_2}{E_1} = \dfrac{d_1^2}{d_2^2}$

   $\dfrac{E_2}{1330 \text{ lx}} = \dfrac{(8.00 \text{ m})^2}{(2.00 \text{ m})^2} = \left(\dfrac{8}{2}\right)^2 = 4^2 = 16$

   $E_2 = 16(1330 \text{ lx}) = 21\ 300 \text{ lx}$

9. What wavelengths of visible light are reinforced when white light is reflected from a soap film 176 nm thick?

   A light wave of wavelength λ is reinforced by a thin film of thickness $\dfrac{n\lambda}{4}$, where n is an odd integer.

   Thickness = $\dfrac{n\lambda}{4}$, or $\lambda = \dfrac{4 \times \text{thickness}}{n}$

   For $n = 1$, $\lambda = 4(176 \text{ nm}) = 682 \text{ nm}$, a wavelength in the red part of the visible spectrum

   For $n = 3$, $\lambda = \dfrac{4}{3}(176 \text{ nm}) = 235 \text{ nm}$,

   a wavelength in the ultraviolet spectrum

   This and all subsequent wavelengths are outside the visible spectrum, so, 682 nm is the only visible wavelength reinforced.

Chapter 17

1. A ray of light in air strikes the surface of a liquid at an angle of 65° with the normal. The refracted ray is at an angle of 42° with the normal. What is the index of refraction of this liquid?

   Applying Snell's law,

   Index of refraction = $n = \dfrac{\sin \theta_i}{\sin \theta_r}$

   $n = \dfrac{\sin 65°}{\sin 42°} = 1.35$

2. Lead(II) oxide is commonly added to glass to increase its index of refraction. A typical leaded glass has an index of refraction of 1.81. What is the angle of refraction of a light ray in air that is incident on this type of glass at an angle of 32.5°?

   Applying Snell's law,

   Index of refraction = $n = \dfrac{\sin \theta_i}{\sin \theta_r}$

   $\sin \theta_r = \dfrac{\sin \theta_i}{n} = \dfrac{\sin 32.5°}{1.81} = 0.2969$

   $\theta_r = 17.3°$

3. A layer of the solvent toluene is floating on water in a glass container. A ray of light passing through the water is incident upon the toluene layer at an angle of 58.3°. The angle of the refracted beam in the toluene is 49.0°. Calculate the index of refraction of toluene.

   Applying the general form of Snell's law

   $n_i \sin \theta_i = n_r \sin \theta_r$

   $n_r = n_i \dfrac{\sin \theta_i}{\sin \theta_r}$

   $n_r = \dfrac{(1.33)(\sin 58.3°)}{\sin 49.0°}$

   $n_r = 1.50$

4. A ray of light passing through water enters a different material at an incident angle of 27.4° and is refracted so that the angle of refraction is 31.5°. Is the speed of light in the material faster or slower than the speed of light in water? Explain your answer and show your reasoning in mathematical form.

The speed of light in the material is faster than the speed of light in water. The angle of refraction is larger than the angle of incidence, indicating that the ray was refracted away from the normal. This happens when light passes into a material having a lower index of refraction than the medium in which it had been traveling.

Velocity of light in a substance, $v_{substance}$, is given by

$$v_{substance} = \frac{c}{n_{substance}}$$

So, an inverse relationship exists between $v_{substance}$ and $n_{substance}$. Therefore, as $n_{substance}$ decreases, $v_{substance}$ increases.

5. The index of refraction of the polycarbonate plastic from which CDs and DVDs are made is 1.55. What is the speed of light as it passes through the plastic?

$$v_{substance} = \frac{c}{n_{substance}}$$

$$v_{polycarbonate} = \frac{c}{n_{polycarbonate}}$$

$$= \frac{3.00 \times 10^8 \text{ m/s}}{1.55}$$

$$= 1.94 \times 10^8 \text{ m/s}$$

6. A certain ray of green light has a wavelength of 5.40×10^{-7} m in air. What is the wavelength of this light as it passes through a diamond, $n_{diamond} = 2.42$? Consider how the frequency (color) of the light affected as it travels in the diamond.

Velocity and wavelength of waves are related by the equation, $v = \lambda f$.

Solving for frequency, $f = \frac{v}{\lambda}$.

For the light wave in two different media, air and diamond:

$$f_{air} = \frac{v_{air}}{\lambda_{air}} \text{ and } f_{diamond} = \frac{v_{diamond}}{\lambda_{diamond}}$$

Express the velocity of light in a diamond by using the equation,

$$v_{substance} = \frac{c}{n_{substance}}$$

$$v_{diamond} = \frac{c}{n_{diamond}}$$

Substitute $\frac{c}{n_{diamond}}$ for $v_{diamond}$ in the previous expression.

$$\lambda_{diamond} = \frac{\left(\frac{c}{n_{diamond}}\right)\lambda_{air}}{v_{air}}$$

At this level of precision, $v_{air} \cong c$, so

$$\lambda_{diamond} = \frac{\lambda_{air}}{n_{diamond}}$$

$$= \frac{5.40 \times 10^{-7} \text{ m}}{2.42} = 2.23 \times 10^{-7} \text{ m}$$

7. What is the critical angle for a light ray passing into air from polystyrene plastic, $n_{polystyrene} = 1.60$?

Applying Snell's law

$$n_i \sin \theta_i = n_t \sin \theta_t$$

$$\theta_i = \text{critical angle} = \theta_c$$

$$n_r = n_{air} \cong 1.00$$

$$\sin \theta_r = \sin 90° = 1$$

$$\sin \theta_c = \frac{(1.00)(\sin 90°)}{n_{polystyrene}} = \frac{1.00}{1.60} = 0.625$$

$$\theta_c = 38.7°$$

8. The critical angle of a material is 45.0°. What is the index of refraction of this material?

$$\sin \theta_c = \frac{(1.00)(\sin 90°)}{n_{material}}$$

$$n_{material} = \frac{(1.00)(\sin 90°)}{\sin \theta_c} = \frac{1.00}{\sin 45°} = 1.41$$

ANSWER KEY

Chapter 18

1. A student views an image of a vase in a plane mirror. The apparent height of the vase's image is 32 cm and the image appears 45 cm behind the mirror. How tall is the actual vase and how far in front of the mirror is the vase?

   With a plane mirror, the size and distance of the virtual image are the same as those of the object.

   $D_o = D_i$ and $h_o = h_i$

   $D_o = 45$ cm and $h_o = 32$ cm

2. A student uses a spherical concave mirror to focus the sun's rays to start a campfire. The sunlight comes to a focus 12.6 cm from the center of the mirror. What is the mirror's radius of curvature?

   A concave mirror focuses parallel rays from the sun at a distance equal to the focal length of the mirror, f. The radius of curvature, r, is twice the focal length.

   $r = 2f = 2(12.6 \text{ cm}) = 25.2$ cm

3. What is the focal length of a spherical, concave mirror that has a radius of curvature of 426 mm?

   $r = 2f$, so $f = \dfrac{r}{2}$

   $f = \dfrac{462 \text{ mm}}{2} = 213$ mm

4. A spotlight has a spherical, concave mirror acting as a reflector. Its radius of curvature is 2.26 m. Where should a bulb be placed so that the mirror reflects a straight beam of parallel rays? Describe the beam that would be produced by the spotlight if the bulb is placed closer to the mirror?

   Parallel rays entering the mirror come to a focus at a distance equal to the focal length, f. Working in reverse, a light source placed at the focal length will refelct as a beam of parallel rays.

   $r = 2f$, so $f = \dfrac{r}{2}$

   $f = \dfrac{2.26 \text{ mm}}{2} = 1.13$ mm

   If the source is placed nearer than the focal length, the mirror can relfect only a diverging beam.

5. A spherical, concave mirror has a radius of curvature of 85.6 cm. A candle is placed on the principal axis 91.0 cm from the center of the mirror. At what distance from the mirror will a real image of the candle form?

   $r = 2f$, so $f = \dfrac{r}{2}$

   $f = \dfrac{85.6 \text{ cm}}{2} = 42.8$ cm

   Apply the lens/mirror equation and solve for image distance, d_i.

   $\dfrac{1}{f} = \dfrac{1}{d_i} + \dfrac{1}{d_o}, \; \dfrac{1}{d_i} = \dfrac{1}{f} - \dfrac{1}{d_o}$

   $\dfrac{1}{d_i} = \dfrac{d_o - f}{fd_o}, \; d_i = \dfrac{fd_o}{d_o - f}$

   $d_i = \dfrac{(42.8 \text{ cm})(91.0 \text{ cm})}{91.0 \text{ cm} - 42.8 \text{ cm}} = 80.8$ cm

6. A flower is placed in front of a concave, spherical mirror at a distance of 0.350 m from the center of the mirror. A real image of the flower is observed at a distance of 0.288 m from the center of the mirror. Calculate the focal length of the mirror.

   Apply the lens/mirror equation and solve for focal length f.

   $\dfrac{1}{f} = \dfrac{1}{d_i} + \dfrac{1}{d_o}$

   $\dfrac{1}{f} = \dfrac{d_o + d_i}{d_o d_i}, \; f = \dfrac{d_o d_i}{d_o + d_i}$

   $f = \dfrac{(0.350 \text{ m})(0.288 \text{ m})}{0.350 + 0.288} = 0.158$ m

7. If the flower in problem 6 is 8.7 cm tall, how tall is the image of the flower?

   $\dfrac{h_i}{h_o} = \dfrac{-d_i}{d_o}, \; h_i = \dfrac{-h_o d_i}{d_o}$

   $h_i = \dfrac{-(8.7 \text{ cm})(0.288 \text{ m})}{0.350 \text{ m}} = -7.2$ cm

   The height is negative because the image is inverted.

Physics: Principles and Problems

8. Most U.S. passenger cars manufactured in recent years have slightly convex side mirrors on the right side. Suppose your car is equipped with a convex mirror that has a radius of curvature of 7.24 m. How far away will a following car appear to be if it is actually 15.5 m away?

$$f_{convex} = \frac{r}{2} = \frac{-7.24 \text{ m}}{2} = -3.62 \text{ m}$$

$$\frac{1}{f} = \frac{1}{d_i} + \frac{1}{d_o}$$

$$\frac{1}{d_i} = \frac{d_o - f}{fd_o}, \; d_i = \frac{fd_o}{d_o - f}$$

$$d_i = \frac{(-3.62 \text{ m})(15.5 \text{ m})}{(15.5 \text{ m}) - (-3.62 \text{ m})} = -2.93 \text{ m}$$

9. A convex lens with a focal length of 16.6 cm is used to form a real image of an object placed 35.0 cm from the lens. The height of the object is 4.5 cm. Calculate the size and distance of the real image that is formed.

$$\frac{1}{f} = \frac{1}{d_i} + \frac{1}{d_o}$$

$$\frac{1}{d_i} = \frac{d_o - f}{fd_o}, \; d_i = \frac{fd_o}{d_o - f}$$

$$d_i = \frac{(16.6 \text{ cm})(35.0 \text{ cm})}{(35.0 \text{ cm}) - (16.6 \text{ cm})} = 31.6 \text{ cm}$$

$$\frac{h_i}{h_o} = -\frac{d_i}{d_o}, \; h_i = \frac{-h_o d_i}{d_o}$$

$$h_i = \frac{-(4.5 \text{ cm})(31.6 \text{ cm})}{35.0 \text{ cm}} = 4.1 \text{ cm}$$

10. The lens of a certain movie projector has a focal length of 22.50 cm. When a frame of film is in place, it is 23.25 cm from the lens. At what distance from the lens would you place a screen in order to receive a focused image? If the image on the film is 28 mm high, how tall is the image formed on the screen?

$$\frac{1}{f} = \frac{1}{d_i} + \frac{1}{d_o}$$

$$\frac{1}{d_i} = \frac{d_o - f}{fd_o}, \; d_i = \frac{fd_o}{d_o - f}$$

$$d_i = \frac{(22.50 \text{ cm})(23.25 \text{ cm})}{(23.25 \text{ cm}) - (22.50 \text{ cm})} = 697.5 \text{ cm}$$

$$= 6.975 \text{ m}$$

$$\frac{h_i}{h_o} = -\frac{d_i}{d_o}, \; h_i = \frac{-h_o d_i}{d_o}$$

$$h_i = \frac{-(28 \text{ mm})(697.5 \text{ cm})}{23.25 \text{ cm}} = 840 \text{ mm}$$

$$= 0.84 \text{ m}$$

11. Since 1838, the diameter of dimes minted in the United States has been standardized at 17.9 mm. A magnifying lens that has a 125-mm focal length is used to view a dime. If the dime is placed 52.5 mm from the lens, what is the size and distance of the virtual image?

$$\frac{1}{f} = \frac{1}{d_i} + \frac{1}{d_o}$$

$$\frac{1}{d_i} = \frac{d_o - f}{fd_o}, \; d_i = \frac{fd_o}{d_o - f}$$

$$d_i = \frac{(125 \text{ mm})(52.5 \text{ mm})}{(52.5 \text{ mm}) - (125 \text{ mm})} = -90.5 \text{ cm}$$

$$h_i = \frac{-(17.9 \text{ mm})(-90.5 \text{ m})}{52.5 \text{ cm}} = 30.9 \text{ mm}$$

12. The lens of a magnifying loupe forms a 30.0-mm image of a 2.2 mm insect when the insect is placed 25 mm from the lens. What is the focal length of this lens?

$$\frac{h_i}{h_o} = \frac{-d_i}{d_o}, \; d_i = \frac{-h_i d_o}{h_o}$$

$$d_i = \frac{-(30.0 \text{ mm})(25 \text{ mm})}{2.2 \text{ mm}}$$

$$= -341 \text{ mm}$$

$$\frac{1}{f} = \frac{1}{d_i} + \frac{1}{d_o}$$

$$\frac{1}{f} = \frac{d_o + d_i}{d_o d_i}, \; f = \frac{d_o d_i}{d_o + d_i}$$

$$f = \frac{(25 \text{ mm})(-341 \text{ mm})}{25 \text{ mm} - 341 \text{ mm}} = 27 \text{ mm}$$

ANSWER KEY

13. A student views a tree that is 27.5 m tall through a concave lens that has a focal length of −70.0 cm. If the tree is 34.0 m away, how tall is the virtual image of the tree?

$$\frac{1}{f} = \frac{1}{d_i} + \frac{1}{d_o}$$

$$\frac{1}{d_i} = \frac{d_o - f}{fd_o}, \quad d_i = \frac{fd_o}{d_o - f}$$

$$d_i = \frac{(-70.0 \text{ mm})(34.0 \text{ m})}{34.0 \text{ m} - (-70.0 \text{ cm})}$$

$$d_i = \frac{(-0.700 \text{ m})(34.0 \text{ m})}{34.0 \text{ m} - (-0.700 \text{ m})} = -0.686 \text{ m}$$

$$\frac{h_i}{h_o} = \frac{-d_i}{d_o}, \quad d_i = \frac{-h_i d_o}{h_o}$$

$$h_i = \frac{-(27.5 \text{ m})(-0.686 \text{ m})}{34.0 \text{ m}} = 0.555 \text{ m}$$

Chapter 19

1. Green light of a certain wavelength is incident upon two slits separated by 2.10×10^{-5} m. A screen is placed 0.800 m from the slits. The distance from the central bright line to the first-order line is 19.9 mm. What is the wavelength of the light?

$$\lambda = \frac{xd}{L}$$

$$\lambda = \frac{(1.99 \times 10^{-2} \text{ m})(2.10 \times 10^{-5} \text{ m})}{0.800 \text{ m}}$$

$$\lambda = 5.22 \times 10^{-7} \text{ m} = 522 \text{ nm}$$

2. A double-slit grating must be calibrated before use. A laser diode emitting light of wavelength 668.2 nm is shined on the slits. On a screen placed 1.000 m away, the first-order line appears 34.3 mm from the central bright line. What is the distance between the slits of the grating?

$$\frac{x}{L} = \frac{\lambda}{d}, \quad d = \frac{\lambda L}{x}$$

$$d = \frac{(668.2 \text{ nm})(1.000 \text{ m})}{34.3 \text{ mm}}$$

Convert all quantities to meters.

$$d = \frac{(6.682 \times 10^{-7} \text{ m})(1.000 \text{ m})}{0.0343 \text{ m}}$$

$$= 1.95 \times 10^{-5} \text{ m}$$

3. Light from a He-Ne laser ($\lambda = 632.8$ nm) strikes a single slit and is diffracted. On a screen placed 0.850 m away, the first dark band appears at a distance of 10.6 mm from the central bright line. What is the width of the slit?

$$\frac{\lambda}{w} = \frac{x}{L}, \quad w = \frac{\lambda L}{x}$$

$$w = \frac{(632.8 \text{ nm})(0.850 \text{ m})}{10.6 \text{ mm}}$$

$$= \frac{(6.328 \times 10^{-7} \text{ m})(0.850 \text{ m})}{0.0106 \text{ m}}$$

$$w = 5.07 \times 10^{-5} \text{ m}$$

4. Monochromatic blue light of unknown wavelength shines on a slit that is 0.052 mm wide. On a screen placed 1.15 m from the slit, the first dark band appears at a distance of 10.1 mm from the central bright line. Calculate the wavelength of the light.

$$\frac{\lambda}{w} = \frac{x}{L}, \quad \lambda = \frac{wx}{L}$$

$$\lambda = \frac{(5.2 \times 10^{-5} \text{ m})(1.01 \times 10^{-2} \text{ m})}{1.15 \text{ m}}$$

$$\lambda = 4.57 \times 10^{-7} \text{ m} = 457 \text{ nm}$$

5. A spectrometer has a grating in which lines are 1.50×10^{-6} m apart. If monochromatic red light having wavelength of 668 nm is shined on the grating, at what angle will the first-order bright line appear?

$$\lambda = d \sin \theta$$

$$\sin \theta = \frac{\lambda}{d} = \frac{6.68 \times 10^{-7} \text{ m}}{1.50 \times 10^{-6} \text{ m}}$$

$$\theta = 26.4°$$

Physics: Principles and Problems

6. A certain spectroscope uses a grating having 1.00×10^4 lines/cm. What wavelength of light will produce a first-order bright line at an angle of 37.5° from the axis?

$1.00 \times 10^4 \dfrac{\text{lines}}{\text{cm}} \times \dfrac{100 \text{ cm}}{\text{m}}$

$= 1.00 \times 10^6 \dfrac{\text{lines}}{\text{m}}$

$d = 1.00 \times 10^{-6}$ m

$\lambda = d \sin \theta$

$\lambda = (1.00 \times 10^{-6} \text{ m})(\sin 37.5°)$

$\lambda = 6.09 \times 10^{-7}$ m = 609 nm

7. A certain spectroscope produces a first-order line at an angle of 42.9° when 668-nm light from a He-Ne laser is used. What is the distance between the lines of the grating?

$\lambda = d \sin \theta, \quad d = \dfrac{\lambda}{\sin \theta}$

$d = \dfrac{6.68 \times 10^{-7} \text{ m}}{\sin 42.9°} = 9.81 \times 10^{-7}$ m

8. Light from a hydrogen discharge tube is shined through a grating that has a line density of 8550 lines/cm. At what angles from the center axis would you expect to find the 486-nm and the 656-nm lines of the hydrogen emission spectrum?

$8550 \dfrac{\text{lines}}{\text{cm}} \times \dfrac{100 \text{ cm}}{\text{m}} = 8.55 \times 10^5 \dfrac{\text{lines}}{\text{m}}$

$d = 1.17 \times 10^{-6}$ m

For $\lambda = 486$ nm $= 4.86 \times 10^{-7}$ m

$\lambda = d \sin \theta$

$\sin \theta_{486 \text{ nm}} = \dfrac{\lambda}{d} = \dfrac{4.86 \times 10^{-7} \text{ m}}{1.17 \times 10^{-6} \text{ m}}$

$\theta_{486 \text{ nm}} = 24.5°$

For $\lambda = 656$ nm $= 6.56 \times 10^{-7}$ m

$\sin \theta_{656 \text{ nm}} = \dfrac{\lambda}{d} = \dfrac{6.56 \times 10^{-7} \text{ m}}{1.17 \times 10^{-6} \text{ m}}$

$\theta_{656 \text{ nm}} = 34.1°$

9. Light from the strong yellow ($\lambda = 589$ nm) emission line of a sodium vapor lamp is shined through a diffraction grating that has a distance of 1.04×10^{-6} m between slits. A screen stands 1.20 m from the grating. At what distance from the center bright line will the first-order bright line appear?

$\lambda = d \sin \theta = \dfrac{xd}{L}$

$x = \dfrac{\lambda L}{d} = \dfrac{(5.89 \times 10^{-7} \text{ m})(1.20 \text{ m})}{1.04 \times 10^{-6} \text{ m}}$

$x = 0.680$ m

Chapter 20

1. How many excess electrons are on a sphere with a charge of -9.20×10^{-17} C?

$n = \dfrac{q}{e} = \dfrac{9.20 \times 10^{-17} \text{ C}}{1.60 \times 10^{-19} \text{ C/electron}}$

$= 575$ electrons

2. Two charges, q_1 and q_2, are separated by a distance, d, and exert a force, F, on each other. Identify what new force will exist if

   a. q_1 is doubled and q_2 is cut in half.

   Coulomb's law: $F = \dfrac{Kq_A q_B}{d_{AB}^2}$

   Initial force: $F = \dfrac{Kq_1 q_2}{d^2}$

   $F_{\text{new}} = \dfrac{K(2q_1)(\frac{1}{2}q_2)}{d^2} = \dfrac{Kq_1 q_2}{d^2}$

   $F_{\text{new}} = F$

   b. q_1 is tripled and q_2 is doubled.

   $F_{\text{new}} = \dfrac{K(3q_1)(2q_2)}{d^2} = \dfrac{6Kq_1 q_2}{d^2}$

   $F_{\text{new}} = 6F$

   c. q_2 is cut in half and d is tripled.

   $F_{\text{new}} = \dfrac{Kq_1(\frac{1}{2}q_2)}{(3d)^2} = \dfrac{Kq_1(\frac{1}{2}q_2)}{9d^2}$

   $= \dfrac{Kq_1 q_2}{18d^2}$

   $F_{\text{new}} = \dfrac{F}{18}$

ANSWER KEY

3. An electric force of 0.030 N acts between two charges which are 7.2 cm apart. Calculate the force acting between the charges if the distance between them is reduced to 1.5 cm.

$$F = \frac{Kq_A q_B}{d_{AB}^2}$$

$F_1 = 0.030$ N; $d_1 = 7.2$ cm; $d_2 = 1.5$ cm

Force varies as $\frac{1}{d^2}$, so

$$\frac{F_2}{F_1} = \frac{d_1^2}{d_2^2} = \frac{(7.2 \text{ cm})^2}{(1.5 \text{ cm})^2} = 23$$

$F_2 = 23F_1 = 23(0.030 \text{ N}) = 0.69$ N

4. Two negative charges of -24 μC each are separated by 6.0 cm. What force exists between the charges?

$$F = \frac{Kq_A q_B}{d_{AB}^2} = \frac{(9.0 \times 10^9 \text{ N·m}^2/\text{C}^2)(-24 \times 10^{-6} \text{ C})(-24 \times 10^{-6} \text{ C})}{(6.0 \times 10^{-2} \text{ m})^2}$$

$= 1.4 \times 10^3$ N; the force is repulsive

5. Two charged spheres are separated by 315 mm. What is the force between them if the charge on one sphere is $+9.6 \times 10^{-7}$ C and the charge on the other sphere is -2.2×10^{-5} C?

$$F = \frac{Kq_A q_B}{d_{AB}^2} = \frac{(9.0 \times 10^9 \text{ N·m}^2/\text{C}^2)(+9.6 \times 10^{-7} \text{ C})(-2.2 \times 10^{-5} \text{ C})}{(315 \times 10^{-3} \text{ m})^2}$$

$= -1.9$ N; the force is attractive

6. Determine the electrostatic force of attraction between a proton and an electron that are separated by 7.5×10^{-8} m.

$$F = \frac{Kq_A q_B}{d_{AB}^2} = \frac{(9.0 \times 10^9 \text{ N·m}^2/\text{C}^2)(+1.60 \times 10^{-19} \text{ C})(-1.60 \times 10^{-19} \text{ C})}{(7.5 \times 10^{-8} \text{ m})^2}$$

$= -4.1 \times 10^{-14}$ N

7. A positive charge of 3.4×10^{-7} C exerts a repulsive force of 9.0 N on a second charge 4.0 cm away. Determine the second charge.

$$F = \frac{Kq_A q_B}{d_{AB}^2}$$

$$q_B = \frac{Fd_{AB}^2}{Kq_A} = \frac{(+9.0 \text{ N})(4.0 \times 10^{-2} \text{ m})^2}{(9.0 \times 10^9 \text{ N·m}^2/\text{C}^2)(+3.4 \times 10^{-7} \text{ C})}$$

$= 4.7 \times 10^{-6}$ C

The force is repulsive, so the charge is positive.

Physics: Principles and Problems

ANSWER KEY

8. An attractive force of 0.87 N exists between a positive charge of 5.0 µC and a negative charge of −1.5 µC. What is the distance between the charges?

$$F = \frac{Kq_A q_B}{d_{AB}^2}$$

$$d_{AB}^2 = \frac{Kq_A q_B}{F} = \frac{(9.0 \times 10^9 \text{ N·m}^2/\text{C}^2)(+5.0 \times 10^{-6} \text{ C})(-1.5 \times 10^{-6} \text{ C})}{-0.87 \text{ N}}$$

$$= 7.8 \times 10^{-2} \text{ m}^2$$

$$d_{AB} = 2.8 \times 10^{-1} \text{ m} = 0.28 \text{ m} = 28 \text{ cm}$$

9. Two identical point charges exert a repulsive force of 6.0×10^{-3} N when separated by a distance of 6.5 cm. Calculate the charge of each.

$$F = \frac{Kq_A q_B}{d_{AB}^2}$$

The two charges are identical, so

$$F = \frac{Kq^2}{d_{AB}^2}, \text{ or } q^2 = \frac{Fd_{AB}^2}{K}$$

$$q = \sqrt{\frac{Fd_{AB}^2}{K}} = \sqrt{\frac{(+6.0 \times 10^{-3} \text{ N})(6.5 \times 10^{-2} \text{ m})^2}{9.0 \times 10^9 \text{ N·m}^2/\text{C}^2}}$$

$$= \pm 5.3 \times 10^{-8} \text{ C}$$

The charges are either both positive or both negative.

10. Two positively charged spheres, A and B, are separated by 0.25 m. The charge on sphere A is one third the charge on sphere B. Find the charge on each sphere if the force of repulsion is 125 N.

$$F = \frac{Kq_A q_B}{d_{AB}^2}$$

$$q_A = \frac{1}{3}q_B, \text{ so } F = \frac{K(\frac{1}{3}q_B)q_B}{d_{AB}^2} = \frac{Kq_B^2}{3d_{AB}^2}$$

$$q_B^2 = \frac{3d_{AB}^2 F}{K}$$

$$q_B = \sqrt{\frac{3d_{AB}^2 F}{K}} = \sqrt{\frac{(3)(0.25 \text{ m})^2(+125 \text{ N})}{9.0 \times 10^9 \text{ N·m}^2/\text{C}^2}}$$

$$= \pm 5.1 \times 10^{-5} \text{ C}$$

$$q_A = \frac{1}{3}q_B = \pm 1.7 \times 10^{-5} \text{ C}$$

Because the force is repulsive, q_A and q_B must both be positively charged or both must be negatively charged.

ANSWER KEY

11. Three particles are placed in a straight line. The left particle has a charge of $+2.0 \times 10^{-5}$ C, the middle particle has a charge of -4.0×10^{-6} C, and the right particle has a charge of $+3.0 \times 10^{-5}$ C. The left particle is 56 mm from the middle particle and the right particle is 42 mm from the middle particle. Find the net force on the left particle.

$q_A = +2.0 \times 10^{-5}$ C; $q_B = -4.0 \times 10^{-6}$ C; $q_C = +3.0 \times 10^{-5}$ C

$d_{AB} = 56$ mm; $d_{BC} = 42$ mm

$d_{AC} = d_{AB} + d_{BC} = 56$ mm $+ 42$ mm $= 98$ mm

$$F_{B \text{ on } A} = \frac{Kq_A q_B}{d_{AB}^2} = \frac{(9.0 \times 10^9 \text{ N} \cdot \text{m}^2/\text{C}^2)(+2.0 \times 10^{-5} \text{ C})(-4.0 \times 10^{-6} \text{ C})}{(56 \times 10^{-3} \text{ m})^2}$$

$= -2.3 \times 10^2$ N

The force is attractive, so it is to the right.

$$F_{C \text{ on } A} = \frac{Kq_A q_C}{d_{AC}^2} = \frac{(9.0 \times 10^9 \text{ N} \cdot \text{m}^2/\text{C}^2)(+2.0 \times 10^{-5} \text{ C})(+3.0 \times 10^{-5} \text{ C})}{(98 \times 10^{-3} \text{ m})^2}$$

$= +5.6 \times 10^2$ N

The force is repulsive, so it is to the left.

$F_{\text{net on } A} = F_{B \text{ on } A} + F_{C \text{ on } A}$

$= 2.3 \times 10^2$ N (right) $+ 5.6 \times 10^2$ N (left)

$= -2.3 \times 10^2$ N (left) $+ 5.6 \times 10^2$ N (left)

$= 3.3 \times 10^2$ N (left)

12. A positive charge of 23 μC is 15 cm directly north of a positive charge of 38 μC. A third positive charge of 71 μC is 45 cm directly west of the 38-μC charge. Determine the net force on the 38-μC charge.

$q_A = +38$ μC; $q_B = +23$ μC; $q_C = +71$ μC

$d_{AB} = 15$ cm; $d_{AC} = 45$ cm

$$F_{B \text{ on } A} = \frac{Kq_A q_B}{d_{AB}^2} = \frac{(9.0 \times 10^9 \text{ N} \cdot \text{m}^2/\text{C}^2)(+38 \times 10^{-6} \text{ C})(+23 \times 10^{-6} \text{ C})}{(15 \times 10^{-2} \text{ m})^2} = +3.5 \times 10^2 \text{ N}$$

The force is repulsive, so it is southward.

$$F_{C \text{ on } A} = \frac{Kq_A q_C}{d_{AC}^2} = \frac{(9.0 \times 10^9 \text{ N} \cdot \text{m}^2/\text{C}^2)(+38 \times 10^{-6} \text{ C})(+71 \times 10^{-6} \text{ C})}{(45 \times 10^{-2} \text{ m})^2} = +1.2 \times 10^2 \text{ N}$$

The force is repulsive, so it is eastward.

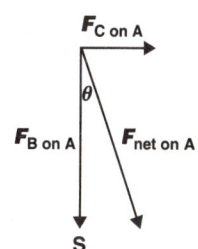

$F_{\text{net on } A} = \sqrt{(+3.5 \times 10^2 \text{ N})^2 + (+1.2 \times 10^2 \text{ N})^2}$

$= +3.7 \times 10^2$ N

$\tan \theta = \dfrac{F_{C \text{ on } A}}{F_{B \text{ on } A}} = \dfrac{+1.2 \times 10^2 \text{ N}}{+3.5 \times 10^2 \text{ N}}$

$\theta = 19°$

$F_{\text{net on } A} = +3.7 \times 10^2$ N, 19° east of south

Physics: Principles and Problems   *Supplemental Problems Answer Key* **113**

Chapter 21

1. A positive test charge of 3.0 μC experiences a force of 0.75 N in an electric field. What is the magnitude of the electric field at the location of the test charge?

   $E = \dfrac{F}{q} = \dfrac{0.75 \text{ N}}{3.0 \times 10^{-3} \text{ C}} = 2.5 \times 10^2 \text{ N/C}$

2. A negative charge of 9.0×10^{-7} C experiences a force of 0.028 N to the left in an electric field. What are the field magnitude and direction?

   $E = \dfrac{F}{q} = \dfrac{0.028 \text{ N}}{9.0 \times 10^{-7} \text{ C}} = 3.1 \times 10^4 \text{ N/C}$

   The test charge is negative so the field direction is to the right, opposite the direction of the force.

3. A charge of 4.00 μC is placed in an electric field of intensity 6.50×10^5 N/C. What is the size of the force on the charge?

   $F = Eq = (6.50 \times 10^5 \text{ N/C})(4.00 \times 10^{-6} \text{ C})$
   $= 2.60 \text{ N}$

4. An electric field with an intensity of 1.5×10^4 N/C exerts a force of 8.1×10^{-3} N on a positive charge. What is the magnitude of the charge?

   $F = Eq$

   $q = \dfrac{F}{E} = \dfrac{8.1 \times 10^{-3} \text{ N}}{1.5 \times 10^4 \text{ N/C}} = 5.4 \times 10^{-7} \text{ C}$

5. Two large, charged parallel plates are 25 cm apart. The magnitude of the electric field between the plates is 1.6×10^3 N/C. What is the electric potential difference between the plates?

   $\Delta V = Ed = (1.6 \times 10^3 \text{ N/C})(0.25 \text{ m})$
   $= 4.0 \times 10^2 \text{ V}$

6. A voltmeter reads 412 V across two charged parallel plates that are 125 mm apart. What is the electric field between them?

   $\Delta V = Ed$

   $E = \dfrac{\Delta V}{d} = \dfrac{412 \text{ V}}{125 \times 10^{-3} \text{ m}} = 3.30 \times 10^3 \text{ N/C}$

7. The potential difference between two charged parallel plates is 720 V. What is the distance between the plates if the electric field between them is 2.4×10^4 N/C?

   $\Delta V = Ed$

   $d = \dfrac{\Delta V}{E} = \dfrac{720 \text{ V}}{2.4 \times 10^4 \text{ N/C}} = 3.0 \times 10^{-2} \text{ m}$
   $= 3.0 \text{ cm}$

8. How much work is required to move a charge of 5.5×10^{-8} C between two points that have a potential difference of 92.5 V?

   $W = q\Delta V = (5.5 \times 10^{-8} \text{ C})(92.5 \text{ V})$
   $= 5.1 \times 10^{-6} \text{ J}$

9. When a charge of 8.50 mC is moved between two points in an electric field, 3.72 J of work are performed. What is the potential difference between the two points?

   $\Delta V = \dfrac{W}{q} = \dfrac{3.72 \text{ J}}{8.50 \times 10^{-3} \text{ C}} = 438 \text{ V}$

10. A positively charged oil drop weighs 2.7×10^{-13} N. It is suspended in an electric field of 4.2×10^5 N/C.

    a. What is the charge on the drop?

    $qE = mg$

    $q = \dfrac{mg}{E} = \dfrac{2.7 \times 10^{-13} \text{ N}}{4.2 \times 10^5 \text{ N/C}}$
    $= 6.4 \times 10^{-19} \text{ C}$

    b. How many electrons is the drop missing?

    $n = \dfrac{q}{e} = \dfrac{6.4 \times 10^{-19} \text{ C}}{1.60 \times 10^{-19} \text{ C/electron}}$
    $= 4 \text{ electrons}$

11. How strong is the electric field that will suspend an oil drop that carries two excess electrons and weighs 6.9×10^{-15} N?

    $q = ne$
    $= (2 \text{ electrons})(1.60 \times 10^{-19} \text{ C/electron})$
    $= 3.20 \times 10^{-19} \text{ C}$

    $qE = mg$

    $E = \dfrac{mg}{q} = \dfrac{6.9 \times 10^{-19} \text{ N}}{3.20 \times 10^{-19} \text{ C}} = 2.2 \times 10^4 \text{ N/C}$

12. An oil drop carrying seven excess electrons is suspended between two charged parallel plates. The plates are separated by a distance of 2.0 cm, and there is a potential difference of 950 V between the plates.

a. What is the sign of the charge on the lower plate?

The oil drop is suspended by an upward force that balances the force of gravity. The oil drop is negatively charged, so the upper plate is positively charged and the lower plate is negatively charged.

b. What is the weight of the suspended oil drop?

$q = ne$
$= (7 \text{ electrons})(1.60 \times 10^{-19} \text{ C/electron})$
$= 1.12 \times 10^{-18} \text{ C}$

$\Delta V = Ed$, so $E = \dfrac{\Delta V}{d}$

$mg = qE = \dfrac{q\Delta V}{d}$

$= \dfrac{(1.12 \times 10^{-18} \text{ C})(950 \text{ V})}{0.020 \text{ m}}$

$= 5.3 \times 10^{-14} \text{ N}$

13. A capacitor with a charge of 0.40 mC has an electric potential difference of 19 V across it. What is the capacitance of the capacitor?

$C = \dfrac{q}{\Delta V} = \dfrac{0.40 \times 10^{-3} \text{ C}}{19 \text{ V}}$
$= 2.1 \times 10^{-5} \text{ C/V} = 21 \ \mu\text{F}$

14. A 120-pF capacitor is connected across a 7500-V potential difference. What is the charge on the capacitor?

$q = C\Delta V = (120 \times 10^{-12} \text{ F})(7500 \text{ V})$
$= 9.0 \times 10^{-7} \text{ C}$

15. What is the voltage across a capacitor with a charge of 8.0×10^{-5} C and a capacitance of 3.0 mF?

$C = \dfrac{q}{\Delta V}$

$\Delta V = \dfrac{q}{C} = \dfrac{8.0 \times 10^{-5} \text{ C}}{3.0 \times 10^{-6} \text{ F}} = 27 \text{ V}$

16. Both capacitor A and capacitor B have the same charge, but the voltage across capacitor A is 12 V while the voltage across capacitor B is 54 V. Compare the capacitances of the two capacitors.

$C = \dfrac{q}{\Delta V}$

The charge, q, is the same on each capacitor.

$C_A = \dfrac{q}{\Delta V_A} \ ; \ C_B = \dfrac{q}{\Delta V_B}$

$\dfrac{C_A}{C_B} = \dfrac{q/\Delta V_A}{q/\Delta V_B} = \dfrac{\Delta V_B}{\Delta V_A} = \dfrac{54 \text{ V}}{12 \text{ V}} = 4.5$

$C_A = 4.5 C_B$

The capacitance of capacitor A is 4.5 times greater than that of capacitor B.

Chapter 22

1. The current through a lamp is 2.50 A.

a. How many coulombs of charge pass through the lamp in 4.00 min?

1 A = 1 C/s

$(2.50 \text{ C/s})(60 \text{ s/min})(4.00 \text{ min})$
$= 6.00 \times 10^2 \text{ C}$

b. How many electrons pass through the lamp in 4.00 min?

$n = \dfrac{q}{e} = \dfrac{6.00 \times 10^2 \text{ C}}{1.60 \times 10^{-19} \text{ C/electron}}$

$= 3.75 \times 10^{21} \text{ electrons}$

2. What power is supplied to a digital clock that operates on a 120-V line and draws 0.0375 A of current?

$P = IV = (0.0375 \text{ A})(120 \text{ V}) = 4.5 \text{ W}$

3. A hair dryer uses 680 W of power while connected to a 120-V outlet. What is the current through the hair dryer?

$P = IV$

$I = \dfrac{P}{V} = \dfrac{680 \text{ W}}{120 \text{ V}} = 5.7 \text{ A}$

Physics: Principles and Problems

Supplemental Problems Answer Key

4. A flashlight uses two 1.5-V batteries. The current through the flashlight bulb is 1.2 A.

   a. How much power does the flashlight use?

   $V = 2(1.5\ V) = 3.0\ V$

   $P = IV = (1.2\ A)(3.0\ V) = 3.6\ W$ or $3.6\ J/s$

   b. How much electric energy is converted when the flashlight is operated for 45 s?

   $E = Pt = (3.6\ J/s)(45\ s) = 1.6 \times 10^2\ J$

5. A resistor is connected to a 9.0-V battery. What is the resistance of the resistor if the current in the circuit is 0.73 A?

   $R = \dfrac{V}{I} = \dfrac{9.0\ V}{0.73\ A} = 12\ \Omega$

6. A lamp with a resistance of 576 Ω is connected to a 120-V source.

   a. What is the current through the lamp?

   $I = \dfrac{V}{R} = \dfrac{120\ V}{576\ \Omega} = 0.21\ A$

   b. What is the power rating of the lamp?

   $P = IV = (0.21\ A)(120\ V) = 25\ W$

7. When a 62-Ω resistor is connected to a battery, the current in the circuit is 0.39 A. What is the voltage of the battery?

   $V = IR = (0.39\ A)(62\ \Omega) = 24\ V$

8. A television is rated at 275 W and operates on a 120-V outlet.

   a. What is the current through the television?

   $I = \dfrac{P}{V} = \dfrac{275\ W}{120\ V} = 2.3\ A$

   b. What is the resistance of the television?

   $R = \dfrac{V}{I} = \dfrac{120\ V}{2.3\ A} = 52\ \Omega$

9. Draw a series-circuit diagram including a 75.0-V battery, an ammeter that reads 833 mA, and a resistor. Label the size of the resistor and indicate the direction of current.

   $R = \dfrac{V}{I} = \dfrac{75.0\ V}{833 \times 10^{-3}\ A} = 90.0\ \Omega$

   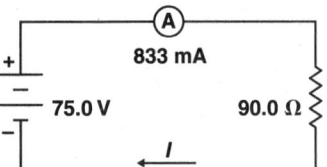

10. A current of 4.6 A is measured through a 7.8-Ω resistor for 1.75 min. How much heat is generated by the resistor?

    $E = I^2Rt$
    $= (4.6\ A)^2(7.8\ \Omega)(1.75\ min)(60\ s/min)$
    $= 1.7 \times 10^4\ J$

11. A 15-W fluorescent lightbulb draws a current of 0.125 A. What is the resistance of the lightbulb?

    $P = I^2R$

    $R = \dfrac{P}{I^2} = \dfrac{15\ W}{(0.125\ A)^2} = 9.6 \times 10^2\ \Omega$

12. A 267-Ω resistor is connected to a 45.0-V battery. How much thermal energy is produced by the resistor in 3.5 min?

    $I = \dfrac{V}{R} = \dfrac{45.0\ V}{267\ \Omega} = 0.169\ A$

    $E = I^2Rt$
    $= (0.169\ A)^2(267\ \Omega)(3.5\ min)(60\ s/min)$
    $= 1.6 \times 10^3\ J$

13. What is the current through a 2250-W electric heater that has an operating resistance of 6.4 Ω?

    $P = I^2R$, so $I^2 = \dfrac{P}{R}$

    $I = \sqrt{\dfrac{P}{R}} = \sqrt{\dfrac{2250\ W}{6.4\ \Omega}} = 19\ A$

14. A computer monitor uses 85 W and is in use 4.0 hours per day. At 11¢ per kWh, what is the cost of operating the monitor for 30 days?

$E = Pt$ = (85 W)(4.0 h/day)(30 days)
　　　= 1.0×10^4 Wh = 1.0×10^1 kWh

Cost = (1.0×10^1 kWh)(11¢/kWh) = $1.10

15. A CD player draws 0.29 A from a 120-V source.

　a. How much power does the CD player use?

　　$P = IV$ = (0.29 A)(120 V) = 35 W

　b. If the CD player is operated for an average of 2.5 hours per day, how much energy in kWh does it consume in one year?

　　$E = Pt$ = (35 W)(2.5 h/day)(365 days/yr)
　　　　= 3.2×10^4 Wh/yr = 32 kWh/yr

16. An electric fan with a resistance of 261 Ω is connected to a 120-V source.

　a. How much current does it draw?

　　$I = \dfrac{V}{R} = \dfrac{120 \text{ V}}{261 \text{ }\Omega} = 0.46$ A

　b. How much power does it use?

　　$P = IV$ = (0.46 A)(120 V) = 55 W

　c. At 12.5¢ per kWh, how much does it cost to operate the fan for 12 hours?

　　$E = Pt$ = (55 W)(12 h) = 660 Wh
　　　　= 0.66 kWh

　　Cost = (0.66 kWh)(12.5¢/kWh) = 8.3¢

17. A 17.0-W compact fluorescent lamp provides as much light as a 60.0-W incandescent lightbulb.

　a. At 11¢ per kWh, what is the cost of operating the compact fluorescent lamp over its lifetime of 1.0×10^4 hours?

　　$E = Pt$ = (17.0 W)(1.0×10^4 h)
　　　　= 1.7×10^5 Wh = 1.7×10^2 kWh

　　Cost = (1.7×10^2 kWh)($0.11/kWh) = $19

　b. At 11¢ per kWh, what is the cost of operating a 60.0-W lightbulb for 1.0×10^4 hours?

　　$E = Pt$ = (60.0 W)(1.0×10^4 h)
　　　　= 6.0×10^5 Wh = 6.0×10^2 kWh

　　Cost = (6.0×10^2 kWh)($0.11/kWh)
　　　　= $66

Chapter 23

1. Three 25.0-Ω resistors are connected in series across a 60.0-V battery.

　a. What is the equivalent resistance of the circuit?

　　$R = R_1 + R_2 + R_3$
　　　= 25.0 Ω + 25.0 Ω + 25.0 Ω = 75.0 Ω

　b. What is the current in the circuit?

　　$I = \dfrac{V}{R} = \dfrac{60.0 \text{ V}}{75.0 \text{ }\Omega} = 0.800$ A

　c. What is the voltage drop across each resistor?

　　$V = IR$ = (0.800 A)(25.0 Ω) = 20.0 V

2. A string of 36 identical holiday lights is connected in series to a 120-V source. The current through the bulbs is 0.40 A.

　a. What is the equivalent resistance of the light string?

　　$R = \dfrac{V}{I} = \dfrac{120 \text{ V}}{0.40 \text{ A}} = 3.0 \times 10^2$ Ω

　b. What is the resistance of each bulb?

　　For each bulb,

　　$R = \dfrac{3.0 \times 10^2 \text{ }\Omega}{36} = 8.3$ Ω

　c. What power is dissipated by the light string?

　　$P = IV$ = (0.40 A)(120 V) = 48 W

ANSWER KEY

3. A lamp with a resistance of 8 Ω is connected across a 24-V battery.

   a. What is the current through the lamp?

   $$I = \frac{V}{R} = \frac{24 \text{ V}}{8 \text{ Ω}} = 3 \text{ A}$$

   b. What resistance must be connected in series with the lamp to reduce the current to 1.6 A?

   Find the equivalent resistance of the series circuit.

   $$R = \frac{V}{I} = \frac{24 \text{ V}}{1.6 \text{ A}} = 15 \text{ Ω}$$

   The resistance to be added is

   $$R = 15 \text{ Ω} - 8 \text{ Ω} = 7 \text{ Ω}$$

4. A 12-Ω resistor and a 28-Ω resistor are connected in series across a battery. The current in the circuit is 0.90 A.

   a. What is the voltage of the battery?

   $$R = R_1 + R_2 = 12 \text{ Ω} + 28 \text{ Ω} = 4.0 \times 10^1 \text{ Ω}$$

   $$V = IR = (0.90 \text{ A})(4.0 \times 10^1 \text{ Ω}) = 36 \text{ V}$$

   b. What is the voltage drop across the 12-W resistor?

   $$V_1 = IR_1 = (0.90 \text{ A})(12 \text{ Ω}) = 11 \text{ V}$$

5. Three resistors are connected in series across a 75-V potential difference. R_1 is 170 Ω and R_2 is 190 Ω. The potential difference across R_3 is 21 V.

   a. Find the current in the circuit.

   For R_1 and R_2 combined,

   $$R_{12} = R_1 + R_2 = 170 \text{ Ω} + 190 \text{ Ω} - 360 \text{ Ω}$$

   $$V_{12} = V_{source} - V_3 = 75 \text{ V} - 21 \text{ V} = 54 \text{ V}$$

   $$I = \frac{V_{12}}{R_{12}} = \frac{54 \text{ V}}{360 \text{ Ω}} = 0.15 \text{ A}$$

   b. Find the resistance of R_3.

   $$R_3 = \frac{V_3}{I} = \frac{21 \text{ V}}{0.15 \text{ A}} = 140 \text{ Ω}$$

6. A 15-V battery and two resistors, R_B of 36 Ω and R_A of 84 Ω, are connected as a voltage divider. What is the voltage across the 36-W resistor?

   $$V_B = \frac{VR_B}{R_A + R_B} = \frac{(15 \text{ V})(36 \text{ Ω})}{84 \text{ Ω} + 36 \text{ Ω}} = 4.5 \text{ V}$$

7. Maria is designing a voltage divider using a 30.0-V battery and a 375-Ω resistor as R_B. What resistor should be used as R_A if the output voltage across R_B is to be 22.5 V?

   $$V_B = \frac{VR_B}{R_A + R_B}, \text{ so } R_A + R_B = \frac{VR_B}{V_B}$$

   $$R_A = \frac{VR_B}{V_B} - R_B = \frac{(30.0 \text{ V})(375 \text{ Ω})}{22.5 \text{ V}} - 375 \text{ Ω}$$

   $$= 5.00 \times 10^2 \text{ Ω} - 375 \text{ Ω} = 125 \text{ Ω}$$

8. A 25-Ω resistor, a 55-Ω resistor, and a 75-Ω resistor are connected in parallel and placed across a 9.0-V battery.

   a. What is the equivalent resistance of the parallel circuit?

   $$\frac{1}{R} = \frac{1}{R_1} + \frac{1}{R_2} + \frac{1}{R_3}$$

   $$= \frac{1}{25 \text{ Ω}} + \frac{1}{55 \text{ Ω}} + \frac{1}{75 \text{ Ω}} = 0.072 \text{ Ω}^{-1}$$

   $$R = 14 \text{ Ω}$$

   b. What is the current through the entire circuit?

   $$I = \frac{V}{R} = \frac{9.0 \text{ V}}{14 \text{ Ω}} = 0.64 \text{ A}$$

   c. What is the current through each branch of the circuit?

   $$I_1 = \frac{V}{R_1} = \frac{9.0 \text{ V}}{25 \text{ Ω}} = 0.36 \text{ A}$$

   $$I_2 = \frac{V}{R_2} = \frac{9.0 \text{ V}}{55 \text{ Ω}} = 0.16 \text{ A}$$

   $$I_3 = \frac{V}{R_3} = \frac{9.0 \text{ V}}{75 \text{ Ω}} = 0.12 \text{ A}$$

ANSWER KEY

9. Suppose that the 25-Ω resistor in problem 8 is replaced by a 45-Ω resistor. Without performing any calculations, describe qualitatively the change in each of the following.

    a. the equivalent resistance of the parallel circuit

    R_1 increases, so the equivalent resistance increases.

    b. the current through the entire circuit

    The equivalent resistance increases, so the current in the circuit decreases.

    c. the current through each branch of the circuit

    The current through R_1 decreases. The currents through the other two branches are unchanged.

10. Two resistors, one 130 Ω and the other 210 Ω, are connected in parallel. The resistors are then connected to a battery. If the current through the entire circuit is 0.31 A, what is the voltage of the battery?

$$\frac{1}{R} = \frac{1}{130 \, \Omega} + \frac{1}{210 \, \Omega}$$

$$R = 8.0 \times 10^1 \, \Omega$$

$$V = IR = (0.31 \text{ A})(8.0 \times 10^1 \, \Omega) = 25 \text{ V}$$

11. Resistors R_1, R_2, and R_3 are connected in parallel. R_1 is 68 Ω and R_2 is 93 Ω. The equivalent resistance of the parallel combination is 26 Ω. What is the resistance of R_3?

$$\frac{1}{R} = \frac{1}{R_1} + \frac{1}{R_2} + \frac{1}{R_3}$$

$$\frac{1}{26 \, \Omega} = \frac{1}{68 \, \Omega} + \frac{1}{93 \, \Omega} + \frac{1}{R_3}$$

$$\frac{1}{R_3} = \frac{1}{26 \, \Omega} - \frac{1}{68 \, \Omega} - \frac{1}{93 \, \Omega}$$

$$R_3 = 77 \, \Omega$$

12. Four identical resistors are connected in parallel. The equivalent resistance of the parallel combination is 4.5 Ω. What is the resistance of each resistor?

$$\frac{1}{R} = \frac{1}{R_1} + \frac{1}{R_2} + \frac{1}{R_3} + \frac{1}{R_4}$$

The four resistors are identical, so $R_1 = R_2 = R_3 = R_4$

$$\frac{1}{R} = \frac{1}{4.5 \, \Omega} = \frac{1}{R_1} + \frac{1}{R_1} + \frac{1}{R_1} + \frac{1}{R_1} = \frac{4}{R_1}$$

$$R_1 = 4(4.5 \, \Omega) = 18 \, \Omega$$

13. A 120-V household circuit that contains a 320-W television, a 1.0×10^2-W lamp, and a 1350-W heater is connected to a 2.0×10^1-A fuse. Will the fuse melt if all three devices are operating simultaneously? Explain.

The power consumption of the three devices is

$$P = 320 \text{ W} + 1.0 \times 10^1 \text{ W} + 1350 \text{ W} = 1770 \text{ W}$$

The maximum allowable power consumption is

$$P = IV = (2.0 \times 10^1 \text{ A})(120 \text{ V}) = 2400 \text{ W}$$

The fuse does not melt.

14. Resistors R_1, R_2, and R_3 have resistances of 37.0 Ω, 22.0 Ω, and 41.0 Ω respectively. R_1 and R_2 are connected in series, and their combination is in parallel with R_3. This arrangement is then placed across a 60.0-V battery.

    a. Draw the circuit diagram.

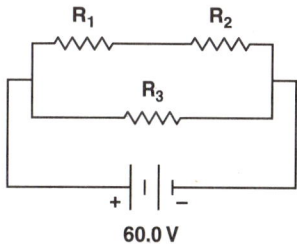

    b. What is the equivalent resistance of the three resistors?

$$R_1 + R_2 = 37.0 \, \Omega + 22.0 \, \Omega = 59.0 \, \Omega$$

$$\frac{1}{R} = \frac{1}{59.0 \, \Omega} + \frac{1}{41.0 \, \Omega}$$

$$R = 24.2 \, \Omega$$

Physics: Principles and Problems   *Supplemental Problems Answer Key* **119**

c. What is the current in the circuit?

$$I = \frac{V}{R} = \frac{60.0 \text{ V}}{24.2 \text{ }\Omega} = 2.48 \text{ A}$$

d. What is the current through R_3?

$$I_3 = \frac{V}{R_3} = \frac{60.0 \text{ V}}{41.0 \text{ }\Omega} = 1.46 \text{ A}$$

e. What is the potential difference across R_1?

$$V_1 = \frac{VR_1}{R_1 + R_2} = \frac{(60.0 \text{ V})(37.0 \text{ }\Omega)}{59.0 \text{ }\Omega}$$
$$= 37.6 \text{ V}$$

15. A 19-Ω resistor is connected in series to a 45-V battery and two 12-Ω resistors that are connected in parallel to each other.

   a. Draw the circuit diagram.

   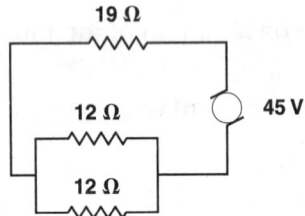

   b. What is the equivalent resistance of the three resistors?

   For the parallel portion,

   $$\frac{1}{R} = \frac{1}{12 \text{ }\Omega} + \frac{1}{12 \text{ }\Omega} = \frac{2}{12 \text{ }\Omega}$$

   $$R = \frac{12 \text{ }\Omega}{2} = 6.0 \text{ }\Omega$$

   For the series-parallel combination,

   $$R = 6.0 \text{ }\Omega + 19 \text{ }\Omega = 25 \text{ }\Omega$$

   c. What is the current in the circuit?

   $$I = \frac{V}{R} = \frac{45 \text{ V}}{25 \text{ }\Omega} = 1.8 \text{ A}$$

   d. What is the current through one of the 12-Ω resistors?

   Both parallel branches contain a 12-Ω resistor, so the current divides equally between the two branches.

   $$I = \frac{1.8 \text{ A}}{2} = 0.90 \text{ A}$$

   e. What is the potential difference across the 19-Ω resistor?

   $$V_1 = IR_1 = (1.8 \text{ A})(19 \text{ }\Omega) = 34 \text{ V}$$

Chapter 24

1. How does the strength of the magnetic field around a wire change if the current in the wire is increased from 0.25 A to 1.75 A?

   The magnetic field strength around the wire is proportional to the current in the wire, so

   $$\frac{B_2}{B_1} = \frac{I_2}{I_1} = \frac{1.75 \text{ A}}{0.25 \text{ A}} = 7.0$$

   $$B_2 = 7.0 \, B_1$$

   The magnetic field is 7.0 times stronger with the 1.75-A current.

2. What is the direction of the force on a current-carrying wire in a magnetic field if the current is toward the right on a page and the magnetic field is out of the page?

   By the third right-hand rule, the force on the wire is directed down the page.

3. A wire 0.80 m long carrying a current of 3.2 A is perpendicular to a 0.15-T magnetic field. What is the force on the wire?

   $$1 \text{ T} = 1 \text{ N/A·m}$$

   $$F = BIL = (0.15 \text{ N/A·m})(3.2 \text{ A})(0.80 \text{ m})$$
   $$= 0.38 \text{ N}$$

4. A wire 375 cm long is perpendicular to Earth's magnetic field. Calculate the force on the wire if the current in the wire is 16 A.

   $$F = BIL = (5 \times 10^{-5} \text{ N/A·m})(16 \text{ A})(3.75 \text{ m})$$
   $$= 3 \times 10^{-3} \text{ N}$$

5. The force on a 0.65 m wire at right angles to a uniform magnetic field is 8.3×10^{-2} N. The current in the wire is 2.1 A. What is the strength of the magnetic field?

   $$F = BIL$$

   $$B = \frac{F}{IL} = \frac{8.3 \times 10^{-2} \text{ N}}{(2.1 \text{ A})(0.65 \text{ m})} = 6.1 \times 10^{-2} \text{ T}$$

ANSWER KEY

6. A wire 7.0 m long is perpendicular to a 2.6-T magnetic field. A 9.5-N force acts on the wire. What is the current in the wire?

$F = BIL$

$I = \dfrac{F}{BL} = \dfrac{9.5 \text{ N}}{(2.6 \text{ T})(7.0 \text{ m})} = 0.52 \text{ A}$

7. A galvanometer has a full-scale deflection when the current is 100.0 μA. If the galvanometer has a resistance of 1.0 kΩ, what should be the resistance of the series (multiplier) resistor to make a voltmeter with a full-scale deflection of 5.0 V?

First find the effective resistance of the galvanometer and the multiplier resistor.

$R = \dfrac{V}{I} = \dfrac{5.0 \text{ V}}{100.0 \times 10^{-6} \text{ A}} = 5.0 \times 10^4 \, \Omega$

$= 5.0 \times 10^1 \text{ k}\Omega$

$5.0 \times 10^1 \text{ k}\Omega = R_{galvanometer} + R_{multiplier}$
$= 1.0 \text{ k}\Omega + R_{multiplier}$

$R_{multiplier} = 49 \text{ k}\Omega$

8. A beam of electrons moves from the back to the front of a room. The beam is deflected rightward, when facing the back of the room, by a magnetic field. What is the direction of the field causing the deflection?

A beam of electrons moving toward the front of a room is equivalent to a beam of positive charges moving toward the back of the room. The third right-hand rule shows that the magnetic field is directed upward, deflecting the beam to the right.

9. A beam of protons travels at right angles to a magnetic field of 4.0×10^{-2} T. The protons have a speed of 5.3×10^6 m/s. What is the size of the force on each proton?

$F = Bqv = (4.0 \times 10^{-2} \text{ T})(1.60 \times 10^{-19} \text{ C})$
$(5.3 \times 10^6 \text{ m/s})$
$= 3.4 \times 10^{-14} \text{ N}$

10. Doubly ionized particles in a beam carry a net positive charge of two elementary charge units. The beam moves at a velocity of 6.1×10^4 m/s perpendicular to a magnetic field of 0.35 T. What is the magnitude of the force acting on each particle?

$F = Bqv = (0.35 \text{ T})(2)(1.60 \times 10^{-19} \text{ C})$
$(6.1 \times 10^4 \text{ m/s})$
$= 6.8 \times 10^{-15} \text{ N}$

11. An electron is traveling at 1.4×10^7 m/s at right angles to a magnetic field. The electron experiences a force of 4.7×10^{-13} N. How strong is the magnetic field?

$F = Bqv$

$B = \dfrac{F}{qv} = \dfrac{4.7 \times 10^{-13} \text{ N}}{(1.60 \times 10^{-19} \text{ C})(1.4 \times 10^7 \text{ m/s})}$

$= 0.21 \text{ T}$

12. A doubly ionized particle experiences a force of 9.2×10^{-14} N when it travels at right angles through a 1.8-T magnetic field. What is the speed of the particle?

$F = Bqv$

$v = \dfrac{F}{Bq} = \dfrac{9.2 \times 10^{-14} \text{ N}}{(1.8 \text{ T})(2)(1.60 \times 10^{-19} \text{ C})}$

$= 1.6 \times 10^5 \text{ m/s}$

13. A magnetic field of 0.50 T acts in a direction due north. An unknown particle travels due east through the field at 8.7×10^5 m/s. The particle experiences an upward force of 2.1×10^{-13} N.

a. Does the particle carry a net positive charge or a net negative charge?

By the third right-hand rule, a positively charged particle moving east through a magnetic field directed north will experience an upward force. Therefore, the particle is positively charged.

Physics: Principles and Problems   *Supplemental Problems Answer Key*

b. How many elementary charges does the particle carry?

$F = Bqv$

$q = \dfrac{F}{Bv} = \dfrac{2.1 \times 10^{-13} \text{ N}}{(0.50 \text{ T})(8.7 \times 10^5 \text{ m/s})}$

$= 4.8 \times 10^{-19}$ C

$n = \dfrac{q}{e}$

$= \dfrac{4.8 \times 10^{-19} \text{ C}}{1.60 \times 10^{-19} \text{ C/elementary charge}}$

= 3 elementary charges

Chapter 25

1. An east-west wire is moved toward the south through a magnetic field that is pointing up, out of Earth. What is the direction of the induced current?

   By the third right-hand rule, the direction of the conventional (positive) current is from east to west.

2. A straight wire, 1.8 m long, moves at 5.0 m/s perpendicular to a magnetic field of strength 6.0×10^{-2} T.

   a. What EMF is induced in the wire?

   $EMF = BLv$
   $= (6.0 \times 10^{-2} \text{ T})(1.8 \text{ m})(5.0 \text{ m/s})$
   $= 0.54$ V

   b. The wire is part of a circuit that has a total resistance of 1.2 Ω. What is the current through the wire?

   $I = \dfrac{V}{R} = \dfrac{0.54 \text{ V}}{1.2 \text{ Ω}} = 0.45$ A

3. A straight wire, 85 cm long, is moved straight up at a speed of 14 m/s through a 0.70-T magnetic field pointed horizontally.

   a. What EMF is induced in the wire?

   $EMF = BLv = (0.70 \text{ T})(0.85 \text{ m})(14 \text{ m/s})$
   $= 8.3$ V

   b. The wire is part of a circuit with a total resistance of 3.0 Ω. What is the current in the circuit?

   $I = \dfrac{V}{R} = \dfrac{8.3 \text{ V}}{3.0 \text{ Ω}} = 2.8$ A

4. An EMF of 0.46 V is induced in a wire 2.5 m long when it is moving perpendicularly across a uniform magnetic field at a speed of 2.0 m/s. What is the strength of the magnetic field?

   $EMF = BLv$

   $B = \dfrac{EMF}{Lv} = \dfrac{0.46 \text{ V}}{(2.5 \text{ m})(2.0 \text{ m/s})} = 9.2 \times 10^{-2}$ T

5. At what speed would a 35-cm length of wire have to move at right angles to a 1.0-T magnetic field to induce an EMF of 1.5 V?

   $EMF = BLv$

   $v = \dfrac{EMF}{BL} = \dfrac{1.5 \text{ V}}{(1.0 \text{ T})(0.35 \text{ m})} = 4.3$ m/s

6. The direction of a 2.8-T magnetic field is northward, 30° above the horizontal. An east-west wire, 4.0 m long, moves horizontally northward at a speed of 1.25 m/s.

   a. What is the vertical component of the magnetic field?

   $B_{vertical} = B \sin 30° = (2.8 \text{ T})(0.50) = 1.4$ T

   b. What EMF is induced in the wire?

   The vertical component of the magnetic field is perpendicular to the motion of the wire, so

   $EMF = B_{vertical}Lv$
   $= (1.4 \text{ T})(4.0 \text{ m})(1.25 \text{ m/s})$
   $= 7.0$ V

7. An AC generator develops a maximum voltage of 315 V.

   a. What is the effective voltage in a circuit placed across the generator?

   $V_{eff} = (0.707)V_{max} = (0.707)(315 \text{ V})$
   $= 223$ V

   b. The resistance of the circuit is 66 Ω. What is the effective current?

   $I_{eff} = \dfrac{V_{eff}}{R} = \dfrac{223 \text{ V}}{66 \text{ Ω}} = 3.4$ A

ANSWER KEY

8. The effective voltage of an AC household outlet is 120 V. The effective current through a lamp connected to the outlet is 0.29 A.

   a. What is the maximum current through the lamp?

   $$I_{max} = \frac{I_{eff}}{0.707} = \frac{0.29 \text{ A}}{0.707} = 0.41 \text{ A}$$

   b. What is the peak power dissipated by the lamp?

   $$P_{AC} = V_{eff}I_{eff} = (120 \text{ V})(0.29 \text{ A}) = 35 \text{ W}$$
   $$P_{max} = 2P_{AC} = 2(35 \text{ W}) = 7.0 \times 10^1 \text{ W}$$

9. A fuse in a 120-V household circuit will melt if the instantaneous current reaches 25.5 A.

   a. What is the largest effective current that the fuse will allow?

   $$I_{eff} = (0.707)I_{max} = (0.707)(25.5 \text{ A}) = 18.0 \text{ A}$$

   b. What is the largest effective power dissipation that the fuse will allow?

   $$P = V_{eff}I_{eff} = (120 \text{ V})(18.0 \text{ A}) = 2.2 \times 10^3 \text{ W or } 2.2 \text{ kW}$$

10. A step-up transformer has 60 turns on its primary coil and 4500 turns on its secondary coil. The primary circuit is supplied with an effective AC voltage of 240 V.

    a. What is the voltage in the secondary circuit?

    $$\frac{V_s}{V_p} = \frac{N_s}{N_p}$$
    $$V_s = \frac{V_p N_s}{N_p} = \frac{(240 \text{ V})(4500)}{60} = 1.8 \times 10^4 \text{ V}$$

    b. The current in the secondary circuit is 0.36 A. What is the current in the primary circuit?

    $$V_p I_p = V_s I_s$$
    $$I_p = \frac{V_s I_s}{V_p} = \frac{(1.8 \times 10^4)(0.36 \text{ A})}{240 \text{ V}} = 27 \text{ A}$$

    c. What power is drawn by the primary circuit? What power is supplied by the secondary circuit?

    $$P_p = V_p I_p = (240 \text{ V})(27 \text{ A}) = 6.5 \times 10^3 \text{ W or } 6.5 \text{ kW}$$

    Check to make sure that the power in both circuits is the same.

    $$P_s = V_s I_s = (1.8 \times 10^4 \text{ V})(0.36 \text{ A}) = 6.5 \times 10^3 \text{ W}$$

    $P_p = P_s$, **as expected.**

11. The primary coil of a transformer has 90 turns. It is connected to a 120-V AC source. Calculate the number of turns on the secondary coil needed to supply these voltages.

    a. 8.0 V

    $$\frac{N_s}{N_p} = \frac{V_s}{V_p}$$
    $$N_s = \frac{N_p V_s}{V_p} = \frac{(90)(8.0 \text{ V})}{120 \text{ V}} = 6 \text{ turns}$$

    b. 44 V

    $$N_s = \frac{N_p V_s}{V_p} = \frac{(90)(44 \text{ V})}{120 \text{ V}} = 33 \text{ turns}$$

    c. 7600 V

    $$N_s = \frac{N_p V_s}{V_p} = \frac{(90)(7600 \text{ V})}{120 \text{ V}} = 5700 \text{ turns}$$

12. A 5.0-kW transformer has an input voltage of 1250 V and an output current of 56 A.

    a. What is the ratio of turns on the secondary coil to turns on the primary coil?

    $$P = V_p I_p$$
    $$I_p = \frac{P}{V_p} = \frac{5.0 \times 10^3 \text{ W}}{1250 \text{ V}} = 4.0 \text{ A}$$
    $$\frac{N_s}{N_p} = \frac{I_p}{I_s} = \frac{4.0 \text{ A}}{56 \text{ A}} = \frac{1.0}{14}$$

    b. Is this a step-up or step-down transformer?

    step-down transformer because $N_p > N_s$

Physics: Principles and Problems

Chapter 26

1. A beam of electrons travels an undeflected path in a Thomson tube. $E = 8.0 \times 10^3$ N/C. $B = 4.5 \times 10^{-2}$ T. What is the speed of the electrons as they travel through the tube?

   $v = E/B = \dfrac{8.0 \times 10^3 \text{ C}}{4.5 \times 10^{-2} \text{ T}} = 1.8 \times 10^5$ m/s

2. An electron moving at 2.0×10^6 m/s moves through a magnetic field of 8.0×10^{-2} T. What is the radius of the electron's path. The mass of an electron is 9.11×10^{-31} kg. $q = 1.6 \times 10^{-19}$.

   $r = \dfrac{mv}{Bq}$

   $= \dfrac{(9.11 \times 10^{-31} \text{ kg})(2.0 \times 10^6 \text{ m/s})}{(8.0 \times 10^{-2} \text{ T})(1.6 \times 10^{-19} \text{ C})}$

   $= 1.4 \times 10^{-4}$ m

3. A magnetic field and an electric field are perpendicular to each other in a Thomson tube. The electric field intensity is 5.0×10^4 N/C, and the intensity of the magnetic field is 3.0×10^{-2} T. What is the speed of the moving particles?

   $v = E/B = \dfrac{5.0 \times 10^4 \text{ N/C}}{3.0 \times 10^{-2} \text{ T}} = 1.7 \times 10^6$ m/s

4. A charged particle is accelerated from rest through a potential difference of 8.0×10^2 V. It enters a magnetic field of 5.0×10^{-2} T. The radius of curvature is 6.0×10^{-2} m.

   a. Calculate the m/q ratio.

   $\dfrac{m}{q} = \dfrac{B^2 r^2}{2V}$

   $= \dfrac{(5.0 \times 10^{-2} \text{ T})^2(6.0 \times 10^{-2} \text{ m})^2}{2(8.0 \times 10^2 \text{ V})}$

   $= 5.6 \times 10^{-9}$ kg/C

   b. If the particle has a charge of 1.6×10^{-19} C, what is its mass?

   $m = q(5.6 \times 10^{-9} \text{ kg/C})$
   $= (1.6 \times 10^{-19} \text{ C})(5.6 \times 10^{-9} \text{ kg/C})$
   $= 9.0 \times 10^{-28}$ kg

5. Alpha particles are accelerated through a potential difference of 8.0×10^2 V. The particles have a mass of 6.68×10^{-27} kg and a charge of twice that of an electron. If the magnetic field is 0.30 T, what is the radius of the path of the particles?

   $\dfrac{q}{m} = \dfrac{2V}{B^2 r^2} \qquad r^2 = \dfrac{2Vm}{B^2 q}$

   $r^2 = \dfrac{2(8.0 \times 10^2 \text{ V})(6.68 \times 10^{-27} \text{ kg})}{(0.30 \text{ T})^2(2)(1.6 \times 10^{-19} \text{ C})}$

   $= 3.71 \times 10^{-4}$ m

   $r = 0.019$ m

6. A proton moves with the speed of 9.0×10^3 m/s through a magnetic field of 4.5×10^{-2} T. The charge on the proton is equal to the charge on the electron only positive. The mass of the proton is 1.67×10^{-27} kg. What is the radius of the circular path?

   $r = \dfrac{mv}{Bq} = \dfrac{(1.67 \times 10^{-27} \text{ kg})(9.0 \times 10^3 \text{ m/s})}{(4.5 \times 10^{-2} \text{ T})(1.6 \times 10^{-19} \text{ C})}$

   $= 2.1 \times 10^{-3}$ m

ANSWER KEY

7. A beam of electrons is bent in a circular path with a radius of 3.0 cm by a magnetic field of 5.0×10^{-4} T. What is the speed of the electrons?

$$v = \frac{Bqr}{m} = \frac{(5.0 \times 10^{-4} \text{ T})(1.6 \times 10^{-19} \text{ C})(0.030 \text{ m})}{9.11 \times 10^{-31} \text{ kg}} = 2.6 \times 10^{6} \text{ m/s}$$

8. A proton moves across a 3.0-T magnetic field. The radius of curvature of the path is 1.5×10^{-2} m.

   a. What is the speed of the proton?

   $$v = \frac{rqB}{m} = \frac{(1.5 \times 10^{-2} \text{ m})(1.6 \times 10^{-19} \text{ C})(3.0 \times 10^{-2} \text{ T})}{1.67 \times 10^{-27} \text{ kg}} = 4.3 \times 10^{4} \text{ m/s}$$

   b. The proton follows a straight line when an electric field is applied at right angles to the magnetic field. What is the strength of the electric field?

   $$E = vB = (4.3 \times 10^{4} \text{ m/s})(3.0 \times 10^{-2} \text{ T}) = 1.3 \times 10^{3} \text{ N/C}$$

9. A lithium ion with a speed of 7.0×10^{5} m/s and a charge of 1.6×10^{-19} C enters the magnetic field of a mass spectrometer. The magnetic field is 0.28 T, and the radius of the ion path is 0.30 m. Find the mass of the lithium ion.

$$m = \frac{Brq}{v} = \frac{(0.28 \text{ T})(0.30 \text{ m})(1.6 \times 10^{-19} \text{ C})}{7.0 \times 10^{5} \text{ m/s}} = 1.9 \times 10^{-26} \text{ kg}$$

10. An electron and a proton move at the same speed as they enter a 3.0×10^{-2} T magnetic field. The electron moves in a circular path of radius 8.0×10^{-3} m. Calculate the radius of the path of the proton.

$$\frac{Bq_e r_e}{m_e} = \frac{Bq_p r_p}{m_p} \quad B_p = B_e, q_p = q_e, \text{ so } \frac{r_e}{m_e} = \frac{r_p}{m_p}$$

$$r_p = \frac{r_e m_p}{m_e} = \frac{(8.0 \times 10^{-3} \text{ m})(1.67 \times 10^{-27} \text{ kg})}{(9.11 \times 10^{-31} \text{ kg})} = 15 \text{ m}$$

11. A mass spectrometer produces a beam of doubly ionized calcium ions. They are first accelerated by a potential difference of 82 V. The magnetic field is 0.090 T. The radius of the path is 6.5×10^{-2} m. Find the mass of the calcium atom as a whole number of proton masses.

$$m = \frac{qB^2 r^2}{2V} = \frac{2(1.6 \times 10^{-19} \text{ kg})(6.5 \times 10^{-2} \text{ m})^2 (0.090 \text{ T})^2}{2(82 \text{ V})} = 6.68 \times 10^{-26} \text{ kg}$$

$$N_p = \frac{m_{Ca}}{m_p} = \frac{6.68 \times 10^{-26} \text{ kg}}{1.67 \times 10^{-27} \text{ kg}}$$

$$= 40 \text{ protons}$$

12. With an accelerating voltage of 73.5 V, a mass spectrometer produces ions with masses of 6.8×10^{-26} kg that move in a circular path with radius of 8.6×10^{-2} m in a 6.5×10^{-2} T magnetic field.

   a. What is the charge on one ion?

   $$q = \frac{2Vm}{B^2r^2}$$

   $$= \frac{2(73.5 \text{ V})(6.8 \times 10^{-26} \text{ kg})}{(6.5 \times 10^{-2} \text{ T})^2(8.6 \times 10^{-2} \text{ m})^2}$$

   $$= 3.2 \times 10^{-19} \text{ C}$$

   b. How many electrons have been removed by the spectrometer to provide the ion?

   $$\frac{3.2 \times 10^{-19} \text{ C}}{1.6 \times 10^{-19} \text{ C/e}} = 2 \text{ e}$$

13. A beam of singly ionized chlorine ions is sent through a mass spectrometer. The values are $B = 0.10$ T, $r = 4.9 \times 10^{-2}$ m, $q = 1.6 \times 10^{-19}$ C, and $V = 33$ V. Find the mass of the chlorine as a whole number of protons.

   $$m = \frac{qB^2r^2}{2V}$$

   $$= \frac{(1.60 \times 10^{-19} \text{ C})(0.10 \text{ T})^2(4.9 \times 10^{-2} \text{ m})^2}{2(33 \text{ V})}$$

   $$= 5.8 \times 10^{-26} \text{ kg}$$

   $$\frac{5.8 \times 10^{-26} \text{ kg}}{1.67 \times 10^{-27} \text{ kg/p}} = 35 \text{ protons}$$

14. In Problem 13 you found the mass of a chlorine isotope. Another chlorine isotope has 37 proton masses. How far from the first isotope would these ions land on the photographic film in the spectrometer?

   Use $r = \frac{1}{B}\sqrt{\frac{2Vm}{q}}$.

   If M equals the number of proton masses

   $$\frac{r_{37}}{r_{35}} = \sqrt{\frac{M_{37}}{M_{35}}}$$

   $$r_{37} = r_{35}\sqrt{\frac{37}{35}} = 5.0 \times 10^{-2} \text{ m}$$

   separation = 2(0.50 m − 0.049 m) = 0.002 m

15. What length antenna would be best to transmit microwaves of wavelength of 2.4 cm?

   L = λ/2 = 4.8 cm/2 = 2.4 cm

16. The radio wave generated by Heinrich Hertz to demonstrate the transmission of radio waves had a frequency of 1.0×10^9 Hz. What length antenna would you use to detect this frequency?

   $c = f\lambda$ $\lambda = c/f = 3.0 \times 10^8$ m/1.0×10^9 Hz
   $$= 0.30 \text{ m}$$

   L = 0.30 m/2 = 0.15 m

Chapter 27

1. When light falls on a photoelectronic surface, the stopping potential required to prevent current through the photocell is 3.5 V.

   a. What is the kinetic energy given to the electrons by the incident light. Give the answer in J and eV.

   $K + W = 0; K = -W$

   $W = qV_0$, so $K = -qV_0$

   $K = -qV_0 = -(-1.60 \times 10^{-19} \text{ C})(3.5 \text{ V})$
   $$= 5.6 \times 10^{-19} \text{ J}$$

   5.6×10^{-19} J(1 eV/1.60×10^{-19} J)
   $$= 3.5 \text{ eV}$$

   b. What is the speed of the electrons?

   $$KE = \frac{1}{2}mv^2$$

   $$v^2 = \frac{2KE}{m} = \frac{2(5.6 \times 10^{-19} \text{ J})}{9.11 \times 10^{-31} \text{ kg}}$$

   $$= 1.23 \times 10^{12} \text{ m}^2/\text{s}^2$$

   $v = 1.1 \times 10^6$ m/s

2. The maximum kinetic energy given to electrons by incident light is 4.5 eV. What is the stopping voltage that prevents electrons from leaving the photocell?

   $K + W = 0; K = -W$

   $W = qV_0$, so $K = -qV_0$

   $K = -qV_0$

   $$V_0 = \frac{-K}{q} = \frac{-4.5 \text{ eV}(1.60 \times 10^{-19} \text{ J/eV})}{-1.60 \times 10^{-19} \text{ C}}$$

   $$= 4.5 \text{ V}$$

ANSWER KEY

3. A certain metal has a threshold frequency of 1.5×10^{14} Hz.

   a. What is the work function of the metal in J and eV?

   $W = hf_0$
   $= (6.626 \times 10^{-34} \text{ J·s})(1.5 \times 10^{14} \text{ Hz})$
   $= 9.9 \times 10^{-20}$ J

   9.9×10^{-20} J/1.60×10^{-19} eV/J = 0.62 eV

   b. The metal is irradiated with light of wavelength 3.0×10^2 nm. What is the kinetic energy of the photoelectrons in eV?

   $K = hc/\lambda - hc/\lambda_0$
   $= \dfrac{1240 \text{ eV·nm}}{3.0 \times 10^2 \text{ nm}} - 0.62 \text{ eV} = 3.5$ eV

4. Light shines on a metal surface in a photocell that has a work function of 1.4 eV. The energy of the most energetic electrons emitted is 0.89 eV. What is the wavelength of the light. In what part of the electromagnetic spectrum is that wavelength?

   $E = hc/\lambda - hf_0$

   $\lambda = \dfrac{hc}{E + hf_0}$

   $= \dfrac{(6.626 \times 10^{-34} \text{ J·s})(3.0 \times 10^8 \text{ m/s})}{(0.89 \text{ eV} + 1.4 \text{ eV})(1.6 \times 10^{-19} \text{ J/eV})}$

   $= 5.4 \times 10^{-7}$ m

   It is in the visible range.

5. The stopping voltage in a photoelectric experiment is 5.3 V. Calculate the kinetic energy of the electrons as they are emitted.

   $K = -qV_0 = -(-1.60 \times 10^{-19} \text{ C})(5.3 \text{ V})$
   $= 8.5 \times 10^{-19}$ J

6. The work function of a metal is 6.4 eV. Calculate the threshold frequency of the metal.

   $W = hf_0$

   $f_0 = \dfrac{W}{h}$

   $= \dfrac{(6.4 \text{ eV})(1.60 \times 10^{-19} \text{ J/eV})}{(6.626 \times 10^{-34} \text{ J/Hz})}$

   $= 1.6 \times 10^{15}$ Hz

7. A metal has a threshold frequency of 3.3×10^{14} Hz. You shine a light with a frequency of 2.0×10^{15} Hz on the metal. Calculate the maximum energy of the ejected electrons.

   $E = hf - hf_0$
   $= 6.626 \times 10^{-34}(2.0 \times 10^{15} \text{ Hz} - 3.3 \times 10^{14} \text{ Hz})$
   $= 1.1 \times 10^{-18}$ J

   1.1×10^{-18} J(1 eV/1.6×10^{-19} J) = 6.9 eV

8. Calculate the final velocity of an electron accelerated from rest across a potential difference of 60.0 V.

   $K = \dfrac{1}{2}mv^2 = qV$

   $v^2 = \dfrac{2qV}{m}$

   $= \dfrac{2(1.60 \times 10^{-19} \text{ C})(60.0 \text{ V})}{9.11 \times 10^{-31} \text{ kg}}$

   $= 2.11 \times 10^{13}$ m^2/s^2

   $v = 4.60 \times 10^6$ m/s

9. Calculate the de Broglie wavelength of a car of mass 1570 kg, traveling at a speed of 35 m/s

   $\lambda = \dfrac{h}{mv} = \dfrac{6.626 \times 10^{-34} \text{ J·s}}{(1570 \text{ kg})(35 \text{ m/s})}$

   $= 1.2 \times 10^{-38}$ m

   Why does the car not exhibit wave properties?
   The wavelength is too small to be observed.

10. A ball with a mass of 0.55 kg is moving with a speed of 7600 m/s. Find the de Broglie wavelength.

    $\lambda = \dfrac{h}{mv} = \dfrac{6.626 \times 10^{-34} \text{ J·s}}{(0.55 \text{ kg})(7.6 \times 10^3 \text{ m/s})}$

    $= 1.6 \times 10^{-37}$ m

11. Compare the de Broglie wavelengths of an electron and a proton, both moving at a speed of 6.0×10^4 m/s.

    $\lambda_e = \dfrac{6.626 \times 10^{-34} \text{ J·s}}{(9.11 \times 10^{-31} \text{ kg})(6.0 \times 10^4 \text{ m/s})}$

    $= 1.2 \times 10^{-8}$ m

    $\lambda_p = \dfrac{6.626 \times 10^{-34} \text{ J·s}}{(1.67 \times 10^{-27} \text{ kg})(6.0 \times 10^4 \text{ m/s})}$

    $= 6.6 \times 10^{-12}$ m

Physics: Principles and Problems   *Supplemental Problems Answer Key*

12. Find the de Broglie wavelength of an electron crossing a potential difference of 2.00×10^4 V in a television set.

$K = qV = \frac{1}{2}mv^2$

$v^2 = \frac{2qV}{m}$

$= \frac{2(1.60 \times 10^{-19} \text{ C})(2.00 \times 10^4 \text{ V})}{9.11 \times 10^{-31} \text{ kg}}$

$= 7.03 \times 10^{15} \text{ m}^2/\text{s}^2$

$v = 8.4 \times 10^7$ m/s

$p = mv = (9.11 \times 10^{-31} \text{ kg})(8.4 \times 10^7 \text{ m/s})$

$= 7.7 \times 10^{-23}$ kg·m/s

$\lambda = \frac{h}{mv} = \frac{6.626 \times 10^{-34} \text{ J·s}}{7.7 \times 10^{-23} \text{ kg·m/s}}$

$= 8.6 \times 10^{-12}$ m

13. The electrons in an electron microscope are accelerated through a potential difference of 5.0×10^4 V. Compare the wavelengths to the wavelengths of visible light.

$qV = \frac{1}{2}mv^2$

$v^2 = \frac{2qV}{m}$

$= \frac{2(1.60 \times 10^{-19} \text{ C})(5.0 \times 10^4 \text{ V})}{9.11 \times 10^{-31}}$

$= 1.76 \times 10^{16} \text{ m}^2/\text{s}^2$

$v = 1.3 \times 10^8$ m/s

$\lambda = \frac{h}{mv} = \frac{6.626 \times 10^{-34} \text{ J·s}}{(9.11 \times 10^{-31} \text{ kg})(1.3 \times 10^8 \text{ m/s})}$

$= 5.6 \times 10^{-12}$ m

The wavelength is about 105 times smaller than visible light.

14. Through what voltage must an electron be accelerated to obtain a de Broglie wavelength of 6.54×10^{-7} m?

$\lambda = \frac{h}{mv}$

$v = \frac{h}{m\lambda}$

$= \frac{6.626 \times 10^{-34} \text{ J·s}}{(9.11 \times 10^{-31} \text{ kg})(6.54 \times 10^{-7} \text{ m})}$

$= 1.1 \times 10^3$ m/s

$V = \frac{mv^2}{2q}$

$= \frac{(9.11 \times 10^{-31} \text{ kg})(1.1 \times 10^3 \text{ m/s})^2}{2(1.60 \times 10^{-19} \text{ C})}$

$= 3.4 \times 10^{-6}$ V

15. Calculate the de Broglie wavelength of a 10.0-g bullet with a velocity of 7.0×10^2 m/s.

$\lambda = \frac{h}{mv} = \frac{6.626 \times 10^{-34} \text{ J·s}}{(1.00 \times 10^{-2} \text{ kg})(7.0 \times 10^2 \text{ m/s})}$

$= 9.5 \times 10^{-35}$ m

ANSWER KEY

Chapter 28

1. What is the radius of the orbital associated with the energy level E_5 of the hydrogen atom?

   $$r = \frac{h^2 n^2}{4\pi^2 K m q^2} = \frac{(6.626 \times 10^{-34} \text{ J·s})^2 (5)^2}{4\pi^2 (9.00 \times 10^9 \text{ N·m}^2/\text{C}^2)(9.11 \times 10^{-31} \text{ kg})(1.6 \times 10^{-19} \text{ C})^2} = 1.32 \times 10^{-9} \text{ m}$$

2. a. Determine the energy associated with the 6th and 8th energy levels of the hydrogen atom.

   $$E_n = -13.6 \text{ eV}\left(\frac{1}{n^2}\right)$$

   $$E_6 = -13.6 \text{ eV}\left(\frac{1}{36}\right) = -0.378 \text{ eV}$$

   $$E_8 = -13.6 \text{ eV}\left(\frac{1}{64}\right) = -0.213 \text{ eV}$$

   b. Determine the energy of the photon emitted as the electron drops from the 8th to the 6th level.

   $$\Delta E = E_8 - E_6 = -0.213 \text{ eV} - (-0.378 \text{ eV}) = 0.165 \text{ eV}$$

   c. Calculate the frequencies of the photons emitted.

   $$\Delta E = hf$$

   $$f = \frac{\Delta E}{h} = \frac{(0.165 \text{ eV})(1.60 \times 10^{-19} \text{ J/eV})}{6.626 \times 10^{-34} \text{ J·s}} = 3.98 \times 10^{13} \text{ Hz}$$

   d. Calculate the wavelength of the photon emitted

   $$\lambda = \frac{c}{f} = \frac{3.00 \times 10^8 \text{ m/s}}{3.98 \times 10^{13} \text{ Hz}} = 7.54 \times 10^{-6} \text{ m}$$

3. a. How much energy must be absorbed to excite an electron from E_2 to E_6?

   $$E_n = -13.6 \text{ eV}\left(\frac{1}{n^2}\right)$$

   $$E_2 = -13.6 \text{ eV}\left(\frac{1}{4}\right) = -3.40 \text{ eV}$$

   $$E_6 = -13.6 \text{ eV}\left(\frac{1}{36}\right) = -0.378 \text{ eV}$$

   $$\Delta E = -0.378 \text{ eV} - (-3.40 \text{ eV}) = 3.02 \text{ eV}$$

   b. What is the wavelength of the energy?

   $$\Delta E = \frac{hc}{\lambda}$$

   $$\lambda = \frac{hc}{\Delta E} = \frac{(6.626 \times 10^{-34} \text{ J·s})(3.00 \times 10^8 \text{ m/s})}{(3.02 \text{ eV})(1.60 \times 10^{-19} \text{ J/eV})} = 4.11 \times 10^{-7} \text{ m}$$

4. An atom drops from −9.32 eV to −7.60 eV.

   a. What is the energy of the photon emitted by the atom?

   $\Delta E = E_2 - E_1 = -7.60 \text{ eV} - (-9.32 \text{ eV})$
   $= -1.72 \text{ eV}$

   b. What is the frequency of the photon?

   $f = \dfrac{\Delta E}{h} = 1.72 \text{ eV} \dfrac{(1.60 \times 10^{-19} \text{ J/eV})}{6.626 \times 10^{-34} \text{ J·s}}$
   $= 4.15 \times 10^{14} \text{ Hz}$

   c. What is the wavelength of the photon?

   $\lambda = \dfrac{c}{f} = \dfrac{3.00 \times 10^8 \text{ m/s}}{4.15 \times 10^{14} \text{ Hz}}$
   $= 7.23 \times 10^{-7} \text{ m}$

5. The wavelength emitted by a hydrogen atom in a down transition from the E_4 energy level is 9.7×10^{-8} m. To which energy level did the electron drop?

   $E = \dfrac{hc}{\lambda}$

   $= \dfrac{(6.626 \times 10^{-34} \text{ J·s})(3.00 \times 10^8 \text{ m/s})}{(9.7 \times 10^{-8} \text{ m})(1.60 \times 10^{-19} \text{ J/eV})}$

   $= 12.8 \text{ eV}$

   $E_4 = -13.6 \text{ eV}\left(\dfrac{1}{16}\right) = -0.850 \text{ eV}$

   $E_4 - E_n = 12.8 \text{ eV}$
   $E_n - E_4 = -12.8 \text{ eV}$
   $= -.850 \text{ eV} - 12.8 \text{ eV}$
   $= 13.6$

   $n = 1$

6. An electron drops from a higher energy level to the E_2 level in hydrogen. The frequency of the light given off is 6.20×10^{14} Hz. What is the energy level from which the electron dropped?

   $E = hf = \dfrac{(6.626 \times 10^{-34} \text{ J·s})(6.20 \times 10^{14})}{1.6 \times 10^{-19} \text{ J/C}}$

   $= 2.57 \text{ eV}$

   $E_2 = -13.6 \text{ eV}\left(\dfrac{1}{4}\right) = -3.40 \text{ eV}$

   $E_n - E_2 = 2.57 \text{ eV}$

   $E_n = E_2 + 2.57 \text{ eV}$
   $= -3.40 \text{ eV} + 2.57 \text{ eV}$
   $= -0.83 \text{ eV}$

   $E_n = -13.6 \text{ eV}\left(\dfrac{1}{n^2}\right)$

   $n^2 = \dfrac{-13.6 \text{ eV}}{E_n}$

   $n^2 = \dfrac{-13.6 \text{ eV}}{-0.83 \text{ eV}} = 16.4$

   $n = 4$

7. Upon absorbing a photon of light of frequency 2.46×10^{15} Hz, an electron in the 1st energy level of a hydrogen atom jumps to the 2nd energy level.

   a. How much energy does the electron have in the second level?

   $\Delta E = hf$
   $= (6.626 \times 10^{-34} \text{ J·s})(2.46 \times 10^{15} \text{ Hz})$
   $= 1.63 \times 10^{-18} \text{ J}$

   b. What is the wavelength of the light emitted by the electron as it returns to the ground state?

   $\lambda = \dfrac{c}{f} = \dfrac{3.00 \times 10^8 \text{ m/s}}{2.46 \times 10^{15} \text{ Hz}}$
   $= 1.22 \times 10^{-7} \text{ m}$

8. What is the maximum wavelength possible for an electron with an orbital radius of 6.20×10^{-11} m? Assume $n = 1$.

   $n\lambda = 2\pi r$

   $\lambda = \dfrac{2\pi r}{n} = \dfrac{2(\pi)(6.20 \times 10^{-11} \text{m})}{1}$

   $= 3.9 \times 10^{-10} \text{ m}$

ANSWER KEY

For questions 9 through 11 use the following table, which shows the energies associated with the first five energy levels of the hydrogen atom.

n	E (eV)
1	−13.6
2	−3.40
3	−1.51
4	−0.850
5	−0.544

9. How much energy in eV must by absorbed by an electron in the 1st energy level to jump to the 3rd energy level?

    $\Delta E = E_3 - E_1 = -1.51 \text{ eV} - (-13.6 \text{ eV}) = 12.1 \text{ eV}$

10. a. Determine the frequency of light emitted as an electron in the third energy level of the excited atom returns to the ground level.

    $\Delta E = E_3 - E_1 = -1.51 \text{eV} - (-13.6 \text{ eV}) = 12.1 \text{ eV}$

    $f = \dfrac{\Delta E}{h} = \dfrac{(12.1 \text{ eV})(1.60 \times 10^{-19} \text{ J/eV})}{6.626 \times 10^{-34} \text{ J} \cdot \text{s}} = 2.92 \times 10^{15} \text{ Hz}$

    b. Determine the wavelength of the light.

    $\lambda = \dfrac{c}{f} = \dfrac{3.00 \times 10^8 \text{ m/s}}{2.92 \times 10^{15} \text{ Hz}} = 1.03 \times 10^{-7} \text{ m}$

11. Calculate the orbital radius associated with the 4th energy level.

    $r = \dfrac{h^2 n^2}{4\pi^2 K m q^2} = \dfrac{(6.626 \times 10^{-34} \text{ J} \cdot \text{s})^2 (4)^2}{4\pi^2 (9.00 \times 10^9 \text{ N} \cdot \text{m}^2/\text{C}^2)(9.11 \times 10^{-31} \text{ kg})(1.60 \times 10^{-19} \text{ C})^2}$

    $= 8.48 \times 10^{-10} \text{ m}$

Chapter 29

1. The forbidden gap in germanium is 0.7 eV. Electromagnetic waves striking the germanium cause electrons to jump from the valence band to the conduction band. What is the longest wavelength of radiation that could excite an electron in this way?

    Recall that $E = \dfrac{1240 \text{ eV} \cdot \text{nm}}{\lambda}$.

    $E = \dfrac{1240 \text{ eV} \cdot \text{nm}}{\lambda}$

    $\lambda = \dfrac{1240 \text{ eV} \cdot \text{nm}}{E} = \dfrac{1240 \text{ eV} \cdot \text{nm}}{0.7 \text{ eV}} = 2 \times 10^3 \text{ nm or } 2 \times 10^{-6} \text{ m}$

    Longer wavelengths do not have enough energy to cause an electron to jump from the valence band to the conduction band.

Physics: Principles and Problems   Supplemental Problems Answer Key

ANSWER KEY

2. A light-emitting diode (LED) produces violet light with a wavelength of 430 nm when an electron moves from the conduction band to the valence band. Find the width of the forbidden gap in eV in this diode.

$$E = \frac{1240 \text{ eV·nm}}{\lambda} = \frac{1240 \text{ eV·nm}}{430 \text{ nm}} = 2.9 \text{ eV}$$

3. How many free electrons exist in a cubic centimeter of calcium? Its density is 1.55 g/cm³, its atomic mass is 40.08 g/mole, and there are two free electrons per atom.

$$\frac{\text{free e}^-}{\text{cm}^3} = \left(\frac{2 \text{ free e}^-}{1 \text{ atom}}\right)\left(\frac{6.02 \times 10^{23} \text{ atoms}}{1 \text{ mol}}\right)$$
$$\left(\frac{1 \text{ mol}}{40.08 \text{ g}}\right)\left(\frac{1.55 \text{ g}}{1 \text{ cm}^3}\right) = 4.66 \times 10^{22} \text{ free e}^-/\text{cm}^3$$

4. Name two elements that could be used as the second dopant used to make a diode, if the first dopant were phosphorus.

   Phosphorus atoms have five valence electrons, so they add electrons to a semiconductor. The second dopant should have only three valence electrons per atom, so it creates holes in the semiconductor. Examples include boron, aluminum, and gallium.

5. The voltage drop across a diode is 2.1 V when it is connected in series to a 275-Ω resistor and a battery, and there is a 36-mA current. What is the battery voltage?

$$V_b = IR + V_d$$
$$= (36 \times 10^{-3} \text{ A})(275 \text{ Ω}) + 2.1 \text{ V}$$
$$= 9.9 \text{ V} + 2.1 \text{ V} = 12.0 \text{ V}$$

6. A diode is connected to a 9.0-V battery through a 1160-Ω resistor. The current in the diode is 7.0 mA. What is the voltage drop across the diode?

$$V_b = IR + V_d$$
$$V_d = V_b - IR$$
$$= 9.0 \text{ V} - (7.0 \times 10^{-3} \text{ A})(1160 \text{ Ω})$$
$$= 9.0 \text{ V} - 8.1 \text{ V} = 0.9 \text{ V}$$

7. The voltage drop across a diode is 1.5 V when it is connected in series to a 785-Ω resistor and a 6.0-V battery. What is the current in the diode?

$$V_b = IR + V_d$$
$$I = \frac{V_b - V_d}{R} = \frac{6.0 \text{ V} - 1.5 \text{ V}}{785 \text{ Ω}}$$
$$= \frac{4.5 \text{ V}}{785 \text{ Ω}} = 5.7 \times 10^{-3} \text{ A or 5.7 mA}$$

Chapter 30

1. Three isotopes of nickel have mass numbers of 56, 59, and 67. The atomic number of nickel is 28. How many neutrons are in the nucleus of each of these isotopes?

   A − Z = neutrons
   56 − 28 = 28 neutrons
   59 − 28 = 31 neutrons
   67 − 28 = 39 neutrons

2. An isotope of carbon has a mass number of 16. How many neutrons are in the nucleus of this isotope?

   A − Z = neutrons
   16 − 6 = 10 neutrons

3. How many neutrons are in the cesium isotope $^{139}_{55}$Cs?

   A − Z = neutrons
   139 − 55 = 84 neutrons

4. The atomic number of gold, Au, is 79. Write the symbols for three isotopes of gold that have 106, 111, and 114 neutrons.

   $^{185}_{79}$Au, $^{190}_{79}$Au, $^{193}_{79}$Au

5. How many neutrons are in the nucleus of an isotope of lead, Pb, that has a mass number of 214?

   A − Z = neutrons
   214 − 82 = 132 neutrons

ANSWER KEY

6. Write the nuclear equation for the transmutation of a radioactive isotope of Polonium, $^{211}_{84}Po$, into the lead isotope $^{207}_{82}Pb$ with the emission of an alpha particle.

   $^{211}_{84}Po \rightarrow {}^{207}_{82}Pb + {}^{4}_{2}He$

7. Write the nuclear equation for the alpha decay of a beryllium isotope, $^{8}_{4}Be$, into a helium isotope $^{4}_{2}He$.

   $^{8}_{4}Be \rightarrow 2\,{}^{4}_{2}He$

8. Write the nuclear equation for the transmutation of a radioactive isotope of actinium, $^{225}_{89}Ac$, into a francium, Fr, isotope by the emission of an alpha particle.

   $^{225}_{89}Ac \rightarrow {}^{221}_{87}Fr + {}^{4}_{2}He$

9. Write the nuclear equation for the transmutation of a radioactive isotope of chlorine, $^{39}_{17}Cl$, into argon, $^{39}_{18}Ar$, by the emission of a beta particle and an antineutrino.

   $^{39}_{17}Cl \rightarrow {}^{39}_{18}Ar + {}^{0}_{-1}e + {}^{0}_{0}\bar{\nu}$

10. A radioactive iron isotope, $^{60}_{26}Fe$, can change into cobalt isotope $^{60}_{27}Co$ by the emission of a beta particle and an antineutrino. Write the nuclear equation.

    $^{60}_{26}Fe \rightarrow {}^{60}_{27}Co + {}^{0}_{-1}e + {}^{0}_{0}\bar{\nu}$

11. Write the nuclear equation for the beta decay of a radioactive isotope of potassium, $^{42}_{19}K$, into an isotope of calcium, Ca.

    $^{42}_{19}K \rightarrow {}^{42}_{20}Ca + {}^{0}_{-1}e + {}^{0}_{0}\bar{\nu}$

Refer to Figure 30-5 on page 699 of your text to solve the following problems.

12. Argon, $^{42}_{16}Ar$, has a half-life of 33 years. If a 4.0-g sample of the argon is produced, what will be the mass of the argon remaining after 99 years?

    99 years = 3(33 years), which is 3 half-lives.

    Since $\frac{1}{2} \times \frac{1}{2} \times \frac{1}{2} = \frac{1}{8}$, there will be

    $\frac{1}{8}$(4.0 g) = 0.050 g remaining

13. A sample of tin, $^{117}_{50}Sn$, has an activity of about 1×10^5 Bq. It has a half-life of 14 days. If a sample was purchased on the first of February, what would be its activity at the end of the month?

    28 days is 2 half-lives

    1×10^5 Bq $\times \frac{1}{2} \times \frac{1}{2} = 2.5 \times 10^4$ Bq

14. An isotope of manganese, $^{53}_{25}Mn$, has a half-life of 2×10^6 years. How would the activity in a rock sample now compare with the activity 5×10^5 years ago?

    5×10^5 is about 0.25 half-lives for the manganese. From Figure 30-5, 13/16 of the original sample remains, so the sample would be 13/16 as active.

15. The mass of a neutron is 1.674×10^{-27} kg.

    a. Find the energy equivalent to the neutron's mass in joules.

    $E = mc^2$
    $= 1.674 \times 10^{-27}$ kg $(3.00 \times 10^8$ m/s$)^2$
    $= 1.51 \times 10^{-10}$ J

    b. Convert this value to eV.

    $(1.51 \times 10^{-10}$ J$)/(1.60 \times 10^{-19}$ J/eV$)$
    $= 9.42 \times 10^8$ eV = 942 MeV

Physics: Principles and Problems

ANSWER KEY

Chapter 31

Use these values for the following problems.

mass of proton = 1.007825 u
mass of neutron = 1.008665 u
1 u = 931.49 MeV

1. A lithium isotope, $^7_3$Li, has a nuclear mass of 7.016005 u.

   a. Calculate the mass defect.

3 protons = 3(1.007825 u) =	3.023475 u
4 neutrons = 4(1.008665 u) =	+4.034660 u
	7.058135 u
mass of nucleus	7.016005 u
	−7.058135 u
mass defect =	−0.042130 u

   b. Calculate the binding energy.

   (931.49 MeV/u)(−0.042130 u) = −39.244 MeV

2. A carbon isotope, $^{14}_6$C, has a nuclear mass of 14.00324 u.

   a. Calculate the mass defect.

6 protons = 6(1.007825 u) =	6.04695 u
8 neutrons = 8(1.008665 u) =	8.06932 u
	14.11627 u
mass of nucleus	14.00324 u
	−14.11627 u
mass defect	−0.11303 u

   b. Calculate the binding energy.

   (931.49 MeV/u)(−0.11303 u) = −105.29 MeV

3. The isotope of chlorine that has 17 protons and 20 neutrons has a mass of 36.96590 u.

   a. Calculate its mass defect.

17 protons = 17(1.007825 u) =	17.13303 u
20 neutrons = 20(1.008665 u) =	20.17330 u
	37.30633 u
mass of nucleus	36.96590 u
	−36.96590 u
mass defect	− 0.34043 u

   b. Find the binding energy.

   (931.49 MeV/u)(−0.34043 u) = 317.11 MeV

ANSWER KEY

4. An isotope of cobalt, $^{60}_{27}$Co, has a mass of 59.93382 u.

   a. Find the mass defect.

27 protons = 27(1.007825 u) =	27.21128 u
33 neutrons = 33(1.008665 u) =	<u>33.28595 u</u>
	60.49723 u
mass of nucleus	59.93382 u
	<u>−60.49723 u</u>
mass defect	− 0.56341 u

   b. Find the binding energy.

   (931.49 MeV/u)(−0.56341 u) = 524.81 MeV

5. The mass of an isotope of iron, $^{56}_{26}$Fe, is 55.93490 u.

   a. Find the mass defect.

26 protons = 26(1.007825 u) =	26.20345 u
30 neutrons = 30(1.008665 u) =	<u>30.25995 u</u>
	56.46340 u
mass of nucleus	55.93490 u
	<u>−56.46340 u</u>
mass defect	− 0.52850 u

   b. Find the binding energy.

   (931.49 MeV/u)(−0.52850 u) = 492.29 MeV

6. The nucleus of a calcium isotope, $^{42}_{20}$Ca, is 41.95863 u.

   a. Calculate the mass defect.

20 protons = 20(1.007825 u) =	20.15650 u
22 neutrons = 22(1.008665 u) =	<u>22.19063 u</u>
	42.34713 u
mass of nucleus	41.95863 u
	<u>−42.34713 u</u>
mass defect	− 0.38850 u

   b. Calculate the binding energy.

   (931.49 MeV/u)(−0.38850 u) = −361.88 MeV

Physics: Principles and Problems

ANSWER KEY

Use Appendix F Table F-6 in the text to complete the following equations.

7. Write the nuclear equation when a radioisotope of francium, $^{221}_{87}$Fr, undergoes alpha decay to form an isotope of astatine, At.

    $^{221}_{87}$Fr → $^{217}_{85}$At + $^{4}_{2}$He

8. Complete the following equation: $^{217}_{85}$At → ? + $^{4}_{2}$He

    $^{217}_{85}$At → $^{213}_{83}$Bi + $^{4}_{2}$He

9. Write the nuclear equation when a radioisotope of thorium, $^{229}_{90}$Th, undergoes alpha decay.

    $^{229}_{90}$Th → $^{225}_{88}$Ra + $^{4}_{2}$He n

10. Write the nuclear equation when a radioactive isotope of platinum, $^{197}_{78}$Pt, undergoes beta decay to form a stable isotope of gold, Au.

    $^{197}_{78}$Pt → $^{197}_{79}$Au + $^{0}_{-1}$e + $^{0}_{0}\bar{\nu}$

11. Write the nuclear equation for the beta decay of a radioactive isotope of cobalt, $^{62}_{27}$Co.

    $^{62}_{27}$Co → $^{62}_{28}$Ni + $^{0}_{-1}$e + $^{0}_{0}\bar{\nu}$

12. Complete the following nuclear equation: $^{55}_{24}$Cr → ? + $^{0}_{-1}$e + $^{0}_{0}\bar{\nu}$.

    $^{55}_{24}$Cr → $^{54}_{25}$Mn + $^{0}_{-1}$e + $^{0}_{0}\bar{\nu}$

13. Write the nuclear equation for the beta decay of a radioisotope of phosphorus, $^{34}_{15}$P.

    $^{34}_{15}$P → $^{34}_{16}$S + $^{0}_{-1}$e + $^{0}_{0}\bar{\nu}$

14. Write the equation for the beta decay of a radioactive isotope of bromine, $^{80}_{35}$Br.

    $^{80}_{35}$Br → $^{80}_{36}$Kr + $^{0}_{-1}$e + $^{0}_{0}\bar{\nu}$